Official Certified SolidWorks Professional (CSWP) Certification Guide with Video Instruction

SolidWorks 2012-2014

David C. Planchard
CSWP & SolidWorks Accredited Educator

Publications

SDC Publications
P.O. Box 1334
Mission, KS 66222
913-262-2664
www.SDCpublications.com
Publisher: Stephen Schroff

ISBN-13: 978-1-58503-899-2
ISBN-10: 1-58503-899-7

Printed and bound in the United States of America.

INTRODUCTION

The **Official Certified SolidWorks® Professional (CSWP) Certification Guide with video instruction, Version 3: 2014, 2013, 2012** is written to assist the SolidWorks user to take and pass the CSWP CORE exam.

It provides CSWP exam tips, hints and information on sample questions and categories that are aligned with each segment of the CSWP CORE exam.

This guide is *not designed to teach a new user* how to use SolidWorks.

Utilize the provided segment videos and model folders to follow along while using the book. Each segment video provides valuable information to successfully pass the CSWP CORE exam.

Copy the CSWP Folder from the DVD to your hard drive. Work directly from your hard drive on the segment chapters in this book. SolidWorks model files (initial and final) for 2012, 2013 and 2014 are provided.

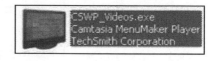

The CSWP Certification exam is offered in three separate segments. The book covers the three segments of the CSWP CORE exam. At this time for SolidWorks World, there is a single three hour CSWP exam only for registered users.

The first segment is not a prerequisite for the second and the second segment is not a prerequisite for the third. You can take the segments in any order.

Each segment covers a different set of disciplines. All segments are timed. You will be tested on data found in the Mass Properties section of SolidWorks. It is important to be familiar with accessing Mass Properties and interpreting them correctly.

The first segment is 90 minutes with six (6) questions. The format is either multiple choice or single fill in the blank. The first question in each segment is typically in a multiple choice format. A total score of 85 out of 115 or better is required to pass the first segment.

You need the exact answer (within 1% of the stated value in the multiple choice section) before you should move on to the next question which is in a single answer format.

If you do not have the exact answer to the first question, you will most likely fail the following questions. This is crucial as there is no partial credit.

In the first segment, you will create a part and modify various dimensions. A question is presented to you in multiple steps and you need to obtain the correct answer at each step to get the question correct. There is no partial credit in the exam.

The Examination Information dialog box states that you are allowed to answer the questions in any order that you prefer. Is this true?

Yes and No! Segment 1 consists of 6 questions. In those six (6) questions there are three major stages to be modeled: Stage 1 (question 1), Stage 2 (question 4) and Stage 3 (question 5). Questions 2, 3 and 6 then ask the user to make a modification to those stages.

Strategically it is best if a user does questions 1, 4 and 5 to model the major stages and compare their Mass Properties to the multiple choice answer. You should be within 1% of the stated value in the multiple choice section before you go back to questions 2, 3 and 6 (single fill in the blank format) to make the changes.

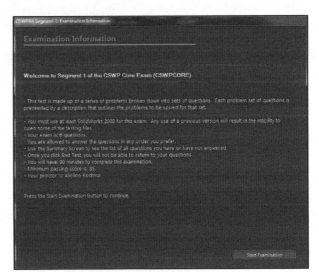

Actual CSWP exam format

When you pass the first segment of the CSWP CORE exam you will receive the following email. Click on the SolidWorks Certification Center hyperlink to login, activate and view your certificate for segment 1.

The second segment of the CSWP CORE exam is 40 minutes with nine (9) questions (11 total but two are instructional pages) divided into two categories. The format is either multiple choice or single fill in the blank. The first question in this segment is typically in a multiple choice format.

The second segment addresses:

- Creating configurations from other configurations

- Modifying configurations using a design table

- Obtaining Mass Properties of various modified configurations

- Modifying features and sketches of an existing part

- Recovering from rebuild errors

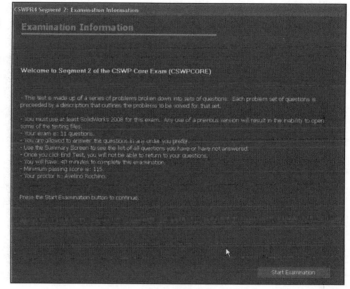

Actual CSWP exam format

A total score of 115 out of 155 or better is required to pass the second segment. When you pass the second segment of the CSWP CORE exam you will receive the following email. Click on the SolidWorks Certification Center hyperlink to login, activate and view your certificate for segment 2.

The third segment is 80 minutes with twelve (12) questions (13 total but one is an instructional page). The format is either multiple choice or single fill in the blank. The first question in each segment is typically in a multiple choice format.

The third segment addresses:

- Creating a simple component and sub-assembly.

- Download parts and assemble components and a sub-assembly into an assembly.

- Utilizing Standard & Advanced (Width, Distance, Angle, etc.) mates.

- Applying Rigid and Flexible states.

- Employing the Interference Detection tool and Collision tool.

- Creating and using a Coordinate System.

- Modifying and replacing components and recovering from mate errors.

- Calculating the center of gravity and mass of a component and assembly.

Actual CSWP exam format

A total score of 140 out of 190 or better is required to pass the third segment. When you pass the third segment of the CSWP CORE exam you will receive the following email. Click on the SolidWorks Certification Center hyperlink to login, activate and view your certificate for segment 3.

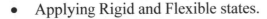

Congratulations David!
You have been issued a certificate in SolidWorks® Virtual Test Center indicating that you have successfully completed the requirements for **Segment 3 of Certified SolidWorks Professional Core**.

CertificateID: (

Visit your certificate area on <u>SolidWorks® Certification Center</u>. Click My Account to access your certificates and exams.

Congratulations,
Avelino Rochino

Once you pass ***all three segments***, you will receive the following email for your CSWP CORE certification in a day or two. Click on the SolidWorks Certification Center hyperlink to login, activate and view your certificate.

Congratulations David!
You have been issued a certificate in SolidWorks® Virtual Test Center indicating that you have successfully completed the requirements for .

CertificateID: (

To download your certificate, visit <u>SolidWorks® Certification Center</u> and click My Account.

Congratulations,
VirtualTester Online

Reference ID:

SolidWorks® is a registered trademark of Dassault Systèmes SolidWorks Corp.

Valid Certificates						
	Certificate ID	Certificate	Issued By	Issued On		
	C-B9F	Segment 2 of Certified SolidWorks Pr...	Avelino Rochino, SolidWorks Corporation	02/14/2011		
	C-UP7	Segment 1 of Certified SolidWorks Pr...	Avelino Rochino, SolidWorks Corporation	02/13/2011		
	C-HV	Segment 3 of Certified SolidWorks Pr...	Avelino Rochino, SolidWorks Corporation	03/06/2011		
☆	C-VU	Certified SolidWorks Professional – C...	VirtualTester Online, Tangix Design & Devel...	03/06/2011		

Print out your CSWP certification as illustrated.

🔆 If you fail a segment of the exam, you need to wait 14 days until you can retake that same segment. In that time, you can take another segment.

During the exam, SolidWorks provides the ability to click on a detail view to obtain additional details and dimensions.

FeatureManager names were changed through various revisions of SolidWorks. Example: Extrude1 vs. Boss-Extrude1. These changes do not affect the models or answers in this book.

Prior to SolidWorks 2013, a method commonly used to define variables for CSWP exam problems was to use Linked Values. Linked Values, also called linked dimensions, connect two or more dimensions without using equations or relations. Linked Values can still be used today in SolidWorks 2013 and SolidWorks 2014. The method to apply Linked Values is described in videos included in the book's DVD.

For SolidWorks 2013 and SolidWorks 2014, the method of using Global Variables to define variables for the CSWP exam problems is documented in the book. Global Variables are easier to find and change in the CSWP exam problems.

Goals

The primary goal is not only to help you pass the CSWP CORE exam, but also to ensure that you understand and comprehend the concepts and implementation details of the process.

The second goal is to provide the most comprehensive coverage of CSWP CORE exam related topics available, without too much coverage of topics not on the exam.

The third and ultimate goal is to get you from where you are today to the point that you can confidently pass all three segments of the CSWP CORE exam. You must work quickly and accurately.

CSWP Audience

The intended audience for this book and the CSWP exam is a person who has passed the CSWA exam and who has 8 or more months of SolidWorks training and usage.

The CSWA exam is not a prerequisite for the CSWP exam if you are a commercial user in industry. For students that take the CSWP exam through their school, you must first pass the CSWA exam.

About the Author

David Planchard is the founder of D&M Education LLC. Before starting D&M Education, he spent over 27 years in industry and academia holding various engineering, marketing, and teaching positions. He holds five U.S. patents. He has published and authored numerous papers on Machine Design, Product Design, Mechanics of Materials, and Solid Modeling. He is an active member of the SolidWorks Users Group and the American Society of Engineering Education (ASEE). David holds a BSME, MSM with the following professional certifications: CCAI, CCNP, CSDA, CSWSA-FEA, CSWP, CSWP-DRWT and SolidWorks Accredited Educator. David is a SolidWorks Solution Partner, an Adjunct Faculty member and the SAE advisor at Worcester Polytechnic Institute in the Mechanical Engineering department.

David Planchard is the author of the following books:

- **SolidWorks® 2014 Reference Guide**, 2013, 2012, 2011, 2010, 2009 and 2008

- **Assembly Modeling with SolidWorks® 2012,** 2010, 2008, 2006, 2005-2004, 2003 and 2001Plus

- **Drawing and Detailing with SolidWorks® 2014**, 2012, 2010, 2009, 2008, 2007, 2006, 2005, 2004, 2003, 2002 and 2001/2001Plus

- **Engineering Design with SolidWorks® and video instruction 2014**, 2013, 2012, 2011, 2010, 2009, 2008, 2007, 2006, 2005, 2004, 2003, 2001Plus, 2001 and 1999

- **Engineering Graphics with SolidWorks® and video instruction 2014**, 2013, 2012, 2011, 2010

- **SolidWorks® 2014 in 5 Hours with video instruction, Version 1**

- **SolidWorks® Tutorial with video instruction 2014**, 2013, 2012, 2011, 2010, 2009, 2008, 2007, 2006, 2005, 2004, 2003 and 2001/2001Plus

- **Official Certified SolidWorks® Associate Examination Guide, Version 4: 2012, 2011, 2010,** Version 3: 2011, 2010, 2009, Version 2: 2010, 2009, 2008, Version 1: 2007

- **Official Certified SolidWorks® Professional (CSWP) Certification Guide with video instruction, Version 3: 2014, 2013, 2012,** Version 2: 2013, 2012, Version 1: 2011, 2010

- **Official Guide to Certified SolidWorks Associate Exams: CSWA, CSDA, and CSWSA-FEA, Version 1: 2013, 2012**

- **Applications in Sheet Metal Using Pro/SHEETMETAL & Pro/ENGINEER**

Acknowledgments

Writing this book was a substantial effort that would not have been possible without the help and support of my loving family and of my professional colleagues. I would like to thank Professor John M. Sullivan, Professor Stephen Nestinger and the community of scholars at Worcester Polytechnic Institute who have enhanced my life, my knowledge, and helped to shape the approach and content to this text.

The author is greatly indebted to my colleagues from Dassault Systèmes SolidWorks Corporation for their help and continuous support: Jeremy Luchini, Avelino Rochino, and Mike Puckett.

SolidWorks Certification has enhanced my skills and knowledge and that of my students. Thanks also to Ian Matthew Jutras (CSWE) who was a technical contributor and reviewer from Worcester Polytechnic Institute and provided insight and invaluable suggestions.

Finally to my wife, who is infinitely patient for her support and encouragement and to our loving daughter Stephanie who supported me during this intense and lengthy project.

Contact the Author

This is the third edition of the **Official Certified SolidWorks Professional (CSWP) Certification Guide with video instruction**. We realize that keeping software application books current is imperative to our customers. We value the hundreds of professors, students, designers, and engineers that have provided us input to enhance our books. We value your suggestions and comments. Please visit our website at **www.dmeducation.net** or contact us directly with any comments, questions or suggestions on this book or any of our other SolidWorks books at dplanchard@msn.com.

References

- SolidWorks Users Guide, SolidWorks Corporation, 2012, 2013, 2014
- ASME Y14 Engineering Drawing and Related Documentation Practices
- Beers & Johnson, Vector Mechanics for Engineers, 6th ed. McGraw Hill, Boston, MA
- Betoline, Wiebe, Miller, Fundamentals of Graphics Communication, Irwin, 1995
- Hibbler, R.C, Engineering Mechanics Statics and Dynamics, 8th ed, Prentice Hall, Saddle River, NJ
- Hoelscher, Springer, Dobrovolny, Graphics for Engineers, John Wiley, 1968
- Jensen, Cecil, Interpreting Engineering Drawings, Glencoe, 2002
- Jensen & Helsel, Engineering Drawing and Design, Glencoe, 1990
- Lockhart & Johnson, Engineering Design Communications, Addison Wesley, 1999
- Olivo C., Payne, Olivo, T, Basic Blueprint Reading and Sketching, Delmar, 1988
- Planchard & Planchard, Drawing and Detailing with SolidWorks, SDC Pub., Mission, KS 2014

Utilize the provided segment videos and model folders to follow along while using the book. Each segment video provides valuable information to successfully pass the CSWP CORE exam.

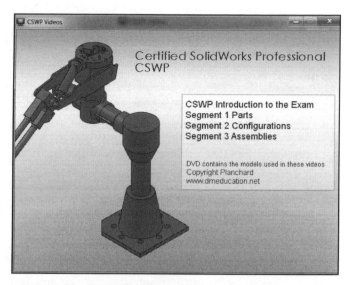

Imported components have imported geometry. Select no on Feature Recognition. Import the geometry as quickly as possible. This is a timed exam.

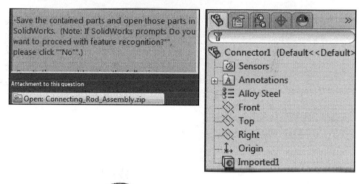

You must use SolidWorks 2008 SP3.1 or newer to take all three segments of the CSWP CORE exam at this time.

There are numerous ways to build the models in this book. A goal is to display different design intents and techniques.

TABLE OF CONTENTS

About the Book

You will find a wealth of information about the three segments of the CSWP CORE exam in this book. The intended audience for this book is a person who has passed the CSWA exam and who has 8 or more months of SolidWorks training and usage.

This guide is *not to teach* you how to use SolidWorks, but is written to provide CSWP exam tips, hints and information on sample questions and categories that are aligned with the exam. The guide is written to help you take and pass the exam.

Utilize the provided segment videos and model folders to follow along while using the book. Each segment video provides value information and tips and tricks to successfully pass the CSWP CORE exam.

Copy the CSWP Folder from the DVD to your hard drive. Work directly from your hard drive on the segment chapters in this book. SolidWorks model files (initial and final) for 2012, 2013 and 2014 are provided.

CSWP Folder 2012	CSWP Folder 2013	CSWP Folder 2014
Name	Name	Name
Segment 1 Final	Segment 1 Final	Segment 1 Final
Segment 1 Initial	Segment 1 Initial	Segment 1 Initial
Segment 2 Final	Segment 2 Final	Segment 2 Final
Segment 2 Initial	Segment 2 Initial	Segment 2 Initial
Segment 3 Final	Segment 3 Final	Segment 3 Initial
Segment 3 Initial	Segment 3 Initial	Segment 3 Final

The book is organized into chapters. Each chapter is focused on a segment of the CSWA CORE exam. This is not a step-by-step book.

Once you *pass all three segments*, you will receive the following email for your CSWP CORE certification in a day or two. Click the hyperlink and visit the SolidWorks Test Center.

Congratulations David!
You have been issued a certificate in SolidWorks® Virtual Test Center indicating that you have successfully completed the requirements for .

CertificateID:

To download your certificate, visit SolidWorks® Certification Center and click My Account.

Congratulations,
VirtualTester Online

Reference ID:

SolidWorks® is a registered trademark of Dassault Systèmes SolidWorks Corp.

Login.

Click Certificates. A list of your Certifications are listed.

Click Validate Certificate.

Enter the requested information. View your valid certificate.

Let the world know that you hold the CSWP Certification.

Good Luck!

Screen shots in the book were made using SolidWorks 2012, 2013 and 2014 SP2 running Windows® 7.

Prior to SolidWorks 2013, a method commonly used to define variables for CSWP exam problems was to use Linked Values. Linked Values, also called linked dimensions, connect two or more dimensions without using equations or relations. Linked Values can still be used today in SolidWorks 2013 and SolidWorks 2014. The method to apply Linked Values is described in videos included in the book's DVD.

Certificate Valid

David Planchard
Certified SolidWorks Professional - Core
Certificate Issued: **03/06/2011**
Validated on: **03/13/2014**

For SolidWorks 2013 and SolidWorks 2014, the method of using Global Variables to define variables for the CSWP exam problems is documented in the book. Global Variables are easier to find and change in the CSWP exam problems

TESTING TIPS

I have collected various testing tips over the years from my colleagues and friends on the SolidWorks Certification exams. Below is a list that may help you prepare and pass the CSWP exam.

1. It is an exam. It is timed. There is no partial credit. Be precise in your work and entering your answers with the correct amount of decimal places. Were you perfect in the sample CSWP exam or on the examples is this book? If not, why? Correct the mistakes before taking the real exam; you will be glad you did.

2. The sample CSWP exam only covers Segment 1 of the CSWP CORE exam. Time yourself on the practice exam. You should be able to finish the sample Segment 1 exam in approximately 60 - 75 minutes.

3. Read up on the contents of the exam that you are not familiar with (collision detection, interference detection, Advanced mates, measure tool, design tables, equations, coordinate locations, replace components, etc.) before you take any segment of the CSWP CORE exam.

4. You will be tested on data found in the Mass Properties section of SolidWorks. It is important to be familiar with accessing Mass Properties and interpreting them correctly.

5. The first question in each segment is usually in a multiple choice format. You need the exact answer (within 1% of the stated value) before you move on to the next question (fill in the blank). If you don't find your answer (within 1%) in the multiple choice single answer format section, recheck your solid model for precision and accuracy.

6. SolidWorks Mass Properties calculates the center of mass for a model. At every instant of time, there is a unique location (x, y, z) in space that is the average position of the systems mass. The CSWP exam asks for center of gravity. For the purpose of calculating the center of mass and center of gravity near to earth or on earth, you can assume that the center of mass and the center of gravity are the same.

7. In Segment 1 of the CSWP CORE exam use Link Values for variables A thru E. Use Equations for X & Y. This will save you time. With Link Values, modify the dimensions not the equations.

8. Create a directory and file structure to save your model during the exam. Create a millimeter, 2 decimal place, part template and assembly template.

9. Take the test on a system you are familiar with. Don't customize your system right before you take the exam.

10. Read all questions before beginning. Pay attention to material changes, origin location, dimensional changes. Note which values indicated by a letter are the ones that will change.

11. Rely only on dimensions and provided information. Do NOT rely on the image provided as a template. Dimensions are changed from test to test so the image used will not be to scale (this is noted in the exam).

12. SolidWorks displays a circle, ellipse or a square around the areas and features that require modification from the original part.

13. Notice where the dimensions are referenced in the drawing views. If the dimensions are referenced from the lower right-hand corner, this is where you should begin with the origin for your Base Sketch (Sketch1).

14. If you use faces versus a dimension, this can help when you need to create a design change to maintain the design intent of the part.

15. Suppress features before you delete them. This will inform you if there are any rebuild or feature errors during modification.

16. A question will be presented to you in multiple steps, and you need to get each step correct to get the final question correct. There is no partial credit on the exam.

17. Always enter the needed decimal places in the answer field even if 0's. Example: 120.00.

18. Always confirm that your math is correct. Use the Measure tool.

19. As a general rule, insert relations before dimensions in a sketch.

20. Fillets are modified often. Use caution when taking the exam.

21. Utilize the split bar to work between the FeatureManager and the ConfigurationManager in Segment 2 of the CSWP CORE exam.

22. In Segment 3 of the CSWP CORE exam, the first component in the assembly should be fixed to the origin or fully defined.

23. You may be required to measure angles between flat surfaces. Be certain to understand the direction, complement or supplement of the required angle.

24. Confirm the position of components inside an assembly when using the Replace Components tool. Apply the Change Transparency tool or a section view to confirm mated component location.

25. SolidWorks will provide a part to create that is not orientated correctly in the assembly. Knowledge of component orientation and changing orientation in an assembly is required along with creating a coordinate system.

26. Save your work frequently and rename saved parts in all segments of the exam.

27. Imported components have imported geometry. Select **NO** on Feature Recognition. Import the geometry as quickly as possible.

28. You must use SolidWorks 2008 SP3.1 or a newer version to take all three segments of the CSWP CORE exam.

29. Relax. Exam anxiety can be a killer. Take a deep breath and enjoy.

There are numerous ways to build the models in this book. A goal is to display different design intents and techniques.

CHAPTER 1 - SEGMENT 1 OF THE CSWP CORE EXAM

Introduction

DS SolidWorks Corp. offers various stages of certification. Each stage represents increasing levels of expertise in 3D CAD design: *Certified SolidWorks Associate CSWA, Certified SolidWorks Professional CSWP and Certified SolidWorks Expert CSWE* along with specialty fields in Drawings, Simulation, Sheet Metal, Surfacing and more.

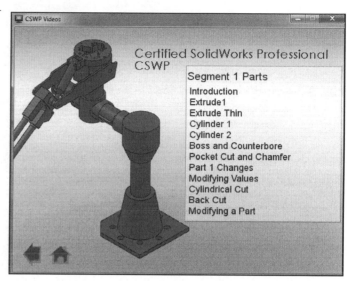

The CSWP Certification exam is offered in three separate segments. The book covers the three separate segments of the CSWP CORE exam. At SolidWorks World, there is a single three hour CSWP exam only for registered users.

The first segment is not a prerequisite for the second and the second segment is not a prerequisite for the third. You can take the segments in any order.

Each segment covers a different set of disciplines. This chapter addresses the first segment of the CSWP CORE exam. All segments are timed. You will be tested on data found in the Mass Properties section of SolidWorks. It is important to be familiar with accessing Mass Properties and interpreting them correctly.

The first segment is 90 minutes with six (6) questions. The format is either multiple choice or single fill in the blank.

The first question in each segment is typically in a multiple choice format. A total score of 85 out of 115 or better is required to pass the first segment.

You should have the exact answer (within 1% of the stated value in the multiple choice section) before you move on to the next question. If you don't have the exact answer of the first question, you will most likely fail the following question. This is crucial as there is no partial credit.

In the first segment, you will create a part and modify various dimensions. A question is presented to you in multiple steps and you need to obtain the correct answer at each step to get the question correct.

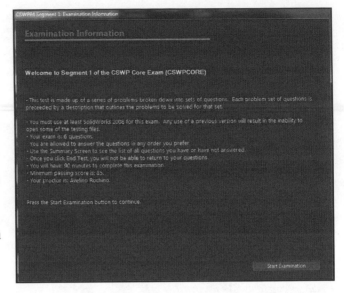

Actual CSWP exam format

The Examination Information dialog box states that you are allowed to answer the questions in any order that you prefer. Is this true?

Yes and No! Segment 1 consists of six (6) questions. In those 6 questions there are three major stages to be modeled: Stage 1 (question 1), Stage 2 (question 4) and Stage 3 (question 5). Questions 2, 3 and 6 then ask the user to make a modification to those stages.

Strategically it is best if a user does questions 1, 4 and 5 to model the major stages and compare their Mass Properties to the multiple choice answer. You should be within 1% of the stated value in the multiple choice section before you go back to questions 2, 3 and 6 (fill in the blank format) to make the changes.

When you pass the first segment of the CSWP CORE exam you will receive the following email. Click on the SolidWorks Certification Center hyperlink to login, activate and view your certificate.

Congratulations David!
You have been issued a certificate in SolidWorks® Virtual Test Center indicating that you have successfully completed the requirements for **Segment 1 of Certified SolidWorks Professional Core.**

CertificateID:

Visit your certificate area on SolidWorks® Certification Center. Click My Account to access your certificates and exams.

Congratulations,
Avelino Rochino

SolidWorks® is a registered trademark of Dassault Systèmes SolidWorks Corp.

For these tasks, review the text and the videos on the DVD that correspond to the competencies you need to know for Segment 1 of the CSWP CORE exam.

Before you start, review the Read and understand an Engineering document section. Engineering drawing views with annotations are presented to you in all segments of the CSWP CORE exam.

Read and understand an Engineering document

What is an Engineering document? In SolidWorks a part, assembly or drawing is referred to as a document. Each document is displayed in the Graphics window.

During the exam, each question will display an information table on the left side of the screen and drawing information on the right. Read the provided information and apply it to the drawing. Various values are provided in each question.

🔅 If you do not find your answer (within 1%) in the multiple choice single answer format section - recheck your solid model for precision and accuracy.

🔅 SolidWorks Mass Properties calculates the center of mass for every model. At every instant of time, there is a unique location (x, y, z) in space that is the average position of the mass in the system. The CSWP exam asks for center of gravity. For the purpose of calculating the center of mass and center of gravity near to earth or on earth, you can assume that the center of mass and the center of gravity are the same.

🔅 SolidWorks views present illustrations that are not proportional to the given dimensions.

Modify the part in SolidWorks.

Unit system: MMGS (millimeter, gram, second)
Decimal places: 2
Part origin: Arbitrary
All holes through all unless shown otherwise.
Material: Aluminium 1060 Alloy
Density = 0.0027 g/mm^3

Modify the part using the following variable values:

A = 140.00
B = 50.00
C = 55 degrees

Note: Assume all unshown dimensions are the same as in the previous question.

What is the overall mass of the part (grams)?

Actual CSWP
exam format

N

Engineering Documentation Practices

2D drawing views are displayed in the CSWP exam.
The ability to interpret a 2D drawing view is required.

- Example 1: *8X Ø.19 EQ. SP*. Eight holes with a
  .19in. diameter are required that are equally (.55in.)
  spaced.

- Example 2: *R2.50 TYP*. Typical radius of 2.50. The
  dimension has a two decimal place
  precision.

DETAIL A
SCALE 2 : 1

- Example 3: ⟱. The Depth/Deep
  ⟱ symbol with a 1.50 dimension
  associated with the hole. The hole
  Ø.562 has a three decimal place
  precision.

- Example 4: *A+40*. A is provided to
  you on the exam. 44mm + A.

⚬ N is a Detail view of the M-M
Section view.

- Example 5: *ØB*. Diameter of B. B is
  provided to you on the exam.

- Example 6: ⓂⓂ. Parallelism.

Build a part from a detailed illustration

Segment 1 of the CSWP CORE exam - First question

Segment 1 of the CSWP CORE exam is one of three sections. In it, you are asked to create and modify a single part. Segments 2 and 3 of the exam require you to download part and component files using the testing client. The question setup in segment 1 is similar to the sample test posted by SolidWorks. Below is the needed information and steps to correctly create the provided model in the sample exam.

View the provided pdf file if needed for this segment.

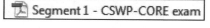

Utilize segment videos and model folders to follow along while using the book. Each segment video provides valuable information to successfully pass the CSWP CORE exam.

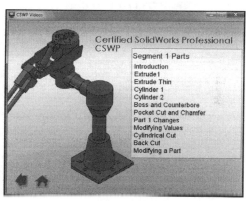

Provided information:

Initial part - Stage 1: Build this part in SolidWorks.

Unit system: MMGS (millimeter, gram, second)

Decimal places: 2

Part origin: Arbitrary

Material: Alloy Steel

Density: 0.0077 g/mm^3

All holes through all unless shown otherwise.

Use the following parameters and equations which correspond to the dimensions labeled in the images:

A = 213 mm

B = 200 mm

C = 170 mm

D = 130 mm

E = 41 mm

F = Hole Wizard Standard: ANSI Metric - Counterbore

    Type: Hex Bolt - ANSI B18.2.3.5M

    Size: M8

    Fit: Close

    Through Hole Diameter: 15.00 mm

Counterbore Diameter: 30.00 mm

Counterbore Depth: 10.00 mm

End Condition: Through All

X = A/3

Y = B/3 + 10mm

Hint #1: The dimensions that are to be linked or updated, and are variable, will be labeled with letters. Any dimensions that are simple value changes from one stage to another will be circled in the images.

Hint #2: To save the most time, make use of linked dimensional values and equations.

Measure the mass of the part.

What is the mass of the part (grams)?

a) 14139.65

b) 14298.56

c) 15118.41

d) 14207.34

HH-HH   JJ-JJ

KK-KK

When you begin segment 1 of the CSWP CORE exam, you will be presented with a variety of drawings and parameters specified in the question. Take your time to first identify the drawing views and to better understand the provided geometry that is needed to create the initial part.

When you create the initial part, think about using Global variables, equations or design tables. This is crucial in this section of the book due to time constraints.

In this section when using SW 2013 & 2014, I use Global Variables and equations. I stay away from design tables.

Note where the variables (A, B, C, D & E) are located in the provided drawing views. F is a Hole Wizard hole.

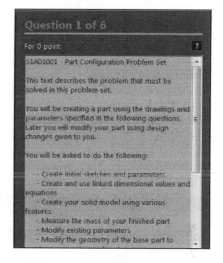

Actual CSWP
exam format

☀ You will see anywhere between 5 to 6 variables and 2 equations in this segment of the exam.

Observe where the dimensions are referenced. In the illustrated example, the dimensions are referenced from the lower right-hand corner. This is where you should begin with the origin of the rectangle for the Base Sketch (Sketch1) in this example.

Most questions ask for a center of gravity or mass in grams. For the former it is crucial that the model is oriented exactly as illustrated. For the latter it does not matter as much, but do not take the chance.

SolidWorks previously used a tool called the Link Value, but this is no longer used. For users familiar with older versions of SolidWorks (2012 or older), the Link Value was what we now think of as a Global Variable. View the provided video on this section to learn more about Link Values.

The text in this section is focused on SolidWorks 2013 and 2014 using Global Variables with the new additional equation drop-down menus in the Modify dialog box and in the Depth box in the PropertyManager.

A Global Variable is just a name assigned to a dimension, a reference measurement, or an entire equation. Global Variables are assigned in the Equations dialog box or in the Modify dimension box as simply the variable name equaling an expression of a value.

KK-KK

Be aware of what is symmetrical and what is different. The two cylinders look the same, but they are not. They have different diameters. It would not make sense to create a pattern or to mirror the two.

Look at the provided variables. Ask yourself what requires a Global Variable in the Equation folder to address speedy part modification in a timed exam?

Understand the provided Hole type.

Based on the provided information, create an Equation folder and input the provided variables.

SolidWorks displays a circle, ellipse or square around the areas and features that require modification from the original part.

Remember, the purpose of this book is not to educate a new or intermediate user on SolidWorks; but to inform you on the types of questions, layout and what to expect when taking the three segments of the CSWP CORE exam.

In this section, you can address part modification through an Equation folder using Global Variables, Equations or by using a design table.

Perform the procedure that you are the most comfortable with.

🔅 The Modify dialog box can accept equations (SW 2013 or newer). You can also use it to create on-the fly Global Variables. To start an equation in the Modify box, start by replacing the numeric value with an = sign in the value box. When you do this, you will see a drop-down menu for functions and file properties. You can also use the dimension entry boxes in the PropertyManager.

$A = 213$ mm

$B = 200$ mm

$C = 170$ mm

$D = 130$ mm

$E = 41$ mm

F = Hole Wizard Standard: Ansi Metric Counterbore

Type: Hex Bolt - ANSI B18.2.3.5M

Size: M8

Fit: Close

Through Hole Diameter: 15.00 mm

Counterbore Diameter: 30.00 mm

Counterbore Depth: 10.00 mm

End Condition: Through All

$X = A/3$

$Y = B/3 + 10$mm

W-W

Let's begin.

1. **Create** a folder to save your models.

2. **Create** a new part.

3. **Set** document properties (drafting standard, units and precision) for the model.

Start with setting the Global variables. The provided variables are:

A = 213 mm

B = 200 mm

C = 170 mm

D = 130 mm

E = 41 mm

4. **Display** the Equation folder in the FeatureManager.

5. **Display** the Equations, Global Variables, and Dimension dialog box.

6. **Enter** the five Global Variables (A, B, C, D & E) as illustrated.

7. **Exit** the dialog box.

View the created Global Variables.

8. **Expand** the Equation folder in the FeatureManager.

Next create the Base Sketch.

9. **Create** Sketch1. Select the Top Plane as the Sketch plane. Sketch1 is the profile for the Extruded Base (Boss-Extrude1) feature. Apply the Corner Rectangle Sketch tool. Click the origin and a position in the upper left section of the Graphics window. Most of the dimensions in the provided drawing view are referenced from this location.

10. **Insert** the horizontal dimension using the Global Variable B(200) from the Modify dialog box.

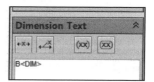

11. **Enter** B for Dimension Text. This will help you keep track of the variables.

12. **Insert** the vertical dimension using the Global Variable A(213) from the Modify dialog box. Sketch1 is fully defined.

13. **Enter A** for Dimension Text.

14. **Display** Primary values. Click View Dimension Names from the Heads-up toolbar. View the results in the Graphics window.

15. **Create** the Extruded Base feature. Boss-Extrude1 is the Base feature. Blind is the default End Condition in Direction 1. Depth = 25mm. Note the direction of the extrude feature.

16. **Assign** Alloy Steel material to the part.

View Dimension Names
Control the visibility of dimension names.

Create the Extrude-Thin feature. The Extrude-Thin feature is controlled by the variable C and two dimensions that are equal (80mm). The height of the feature from the bottom is 95mm.

Start from the Top face and subtract 25mm from 95mm to obtain the correct depth for the Thin-Extrude feature.

17. **Create** Sketch2. Select the Top face. Sketch2 is the profile for the Extrude-Thin feature. Utilize the Line Sketch tool to create a vertical and horizontal line. Utilize the 3 Point Arc Sketch tool to complete the sketch as illustrated.

18. **Add** an Equal relation between the vertical and horizontal line of Sketch2.

19. **Insert** the 80mm dimension on the vertical line.

20. **Insert** the horizontal Global Variable C dimension as illustrated.

21. **Enter** C for Dimension Text.

22. **Insert** the vertical Global Variable C dimension as illustrated.

23. **Enter** C for Dimension Text.

24. **Insert** a horizontal relation between the centerpoint of the arc and the horizontal sketch line end point if needed. The sketch is fully defined and is displayed in black.

25. **Insert** the Extrude-Thin feature. The Extrude-Thin feature is controlled by the Global Variable C and two dimensions that are equal (80mm). The overall height of the part is 95mm. Start from the Top face. Subtract 25mm from 95mm to obtain the correct depth for the Thin-Extrude feature. Click No in the Close Sketch With Model Edges dialog box. You want an open profile. If needed click the Reverse Direction in the Thin Feature box. Enter 15mm for Thickness. Enter 70mm for Depth in the Direction 1 box. Blind is the default End Conditions. Click OK from the Boss-Extrude PropertyManager. Extrude-Thin1 is displayed in the FeatureManager.

At this time - your model should have a mass of **10495.58 grams**. You should have the exact answer (within 1% of the stated value in the multiple choice section) before you move on to the next question.

Density = 0.01 grams per cubic millimeter

Mass = 10495.58 grams

Volume = 1363062.59 cubic millimeters

Surface area = 147734.93 square millimeters

Create the first cylinder (remember the two cylinders are not the same). The first cylinder outside diameter is controlled by equation X. X = A/3. The inside diameter is E = (41mm) and the depth is D = (130mm).

Sample Exam – Initial Part (These images are to be used to answer Questions #1 – 3)

The first cylinder is offset 10mm from the Front Plane or face.

26. **Create** a Plane offset from the Front Plane (front face) 10mm. Plane1 is created.

27. **Create** Skctch3 on Plane1. Sketch a circle with the centerpoint Coincident at the midpoint of the Extrude-Thin1 feature. The dimension is driven by the X equation.

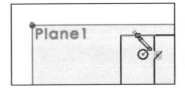

28. **Enter** the equation for X in the Modify dialog box as displayed.

29. **Create** the Extruded Boss feature from Sketch3. Enter the extruded distance of the Global Variable D. Depth D = 130mm. Click Reverse direction if needed as illustrated.

30. **Rebuild** your part. View the results in the Graphics window.

Prior to SolidWorks 2013, a method commonly used to define variables for CSWP exam problems was to use Linked Values. Linked Values, also called linked dimensions, connect two or more dimensions without using equations or relations. Linked Values can still be used today in SolidWorks 2013 and SolidWorks 2014. The method to apply Linked Values is described in videos included in the book's DVD.

For SolidWorks 2013 and SolidWorks 2014, the method of using Global Variables to define variables for the CSWP exam problems is documented in the book. Global Variables are easier to find and change in the CSWP exam problems.

There are numerous ways to build the model in this section. A goal is to display different design intents and techniques.

31. **Create** Sketch4 on the front face of the cylinder to create the Extruded Cut feature. Use the Circle Sketch tool. Click the centerpoint of the Extruded Boss feature for the centerpoint.

32. **Dimension** Sketch4. Insert the Global Variable E. E = 410mm.

33. **Enter** E for Dimension Text.

There are numerous ways to build the model in this section. A goal is to display different design intents and techniques.

34. **Create** an Extruded Cut feature using Sketch4. Select Through All for End Condition to address any future design change for depth.

At this time, your model should have a mass of **12722.39 grams**. You should have the exact answer (within 1% of the stated value in the multiple choice section) before you move on to the next question.

Create the second cylinder, (remember the two cylinders are *not* the same).

The second cylinder outside diameter is controlled by equation Y.

$Y = B/3 + 10mm$.

The inside diameter is $E = (41mm)$.

The depth is $D = (130mm)$.

The second cylinder is offset 10mm from either the Right Plane or right face.

35. **Create** a Plane (Plane2) offset from the Right Plane (right face) 10mm.

36. **Create** Sketch5 on Plane2. Sketch a circle with the centerpoint Coincident at the midpoint of the Extrude-Thin1 feature. The dimension is driven by the Y equation.

37. **Dimension** Sketch5. Enter the equation for Y in the Modify dialog box as displayed.

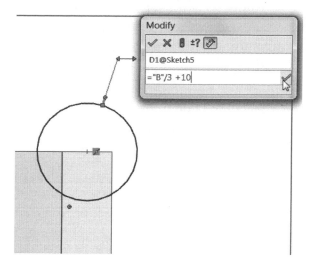

38. **Create** the Extruded Boss feature from Sketch5. Enter the extruded distance of the Global Variable D. Depth D = 130mm. Click Reverse direction if needed as illustrated.

39. **Rebuild** your part. View the results in the Graphics window.

40. Save the part.

41. **Create** Sketch6 on the Right face of the second cylinder to create the Extruded Cut feature. Use the Circle Sketch tool. Click the centerpoint of the Extruded Boss feature for the centerpoint.

42. **Insert** the Global Variable E. E = 41mm.

43. **Enter** E for Dimension Text.

44. **Create** an Extruded Cut feature from Sketch6. Select Through All for End Condition to address any future design change in depth.

At this time, your model should have a mass of **15562.83 grams**.

Always enter the needed decimal places in the answer field.

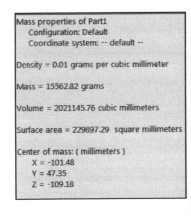

Each segment video provides valuable information to successfully pass the CSWP CORE exam.

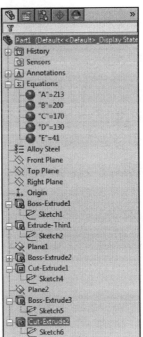

Mass properties of Part1
    Configuration: Default
    Coordinate system: -- default --

Density = 0.01 grams per cubic millimeter

Mass = 15562.82 grams

Volume = 2021145.76 cubic millimeters

Surface area = 229897.29 square millimeters

Center of mass: (millimeters)
    X = -101.48
    Y = 47.35
    Z = -109.18

Create the Extruded Boss, Counterbore and Fillet features on the right side of the model.

45. **Create** Sketch7 on the top face of Boss-Extrude1. Apply the Corner Rectangle tool from the right hand side. Insert an Equal geometric relation. Enter 60mm for dimension.

46. **Create** Boss-Extrude4 from Sketch7. Depth = 10mm. (35mm - 25mm) = 10mm from the provided information in the question.

Create the Counterbore hole using the Hole Wizard feature tool. Remember the provided information.

The Hole Wizard feature tool was modified in SolidWorks 2014. Additional Hole Types and other features were added.

47. **Create** the Counterbore hole using the Hole Wizard on the top face of Boss-Extrude4.

There are numerous ways to build the models in this chapter. A goal is to display different design intents and techniques.

48. **Enter** the provided information in the Hole Specification PropertyManager. This is a Through All End Condition hole.

49. **Create** Sketch9. Use the Centerline Sketch tool with a Midpoint relation to location the center of the hole on the Boss-Extrude4 face. This saves time from creating two dimensions. The hole is complete.

50. **Create** the first Constant radius Fillet (15mm) on the inside corner of the Boss-Extrude4 feature. You can use the Multiple radius fillet option to create all needed fillets, but for design intent and future modifications in the exam; insert two separate fillet features.

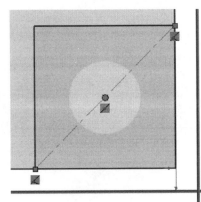

Use caution when taking the CSWP exam. Fillets are modified often. The Fillet PropertyManager was modified in SW 2013 & 2014.

51. **Create** the second Constant radius Fillet (10mm) on the four outside edges of Boss-Extrude1 as illustrated.

At this time, your model should have a mass of **15729.68 grams**.

Mass properties of Part1
    Configuration: Default
    Coordinate system: -- default --

Density = 0.01 grams per cubic millimeter

Mass = 15729.68 grams

Volume = 2042815.84 cubic millimeters

Surface area = 233356.25 square millimeters

Center of mass: (millimeters)
    X = -100.65
    Y = 47.22
    Z = -108.26

Create the Extruded Cut feature (pocket) on the top face of Boss-Extrude1 using the Offset Entities Sketch tool; then create the Chamfer feature.

52. **Create** Sketch10. Use the Offset Entities Sketch (9mm Offset distance) tool. Note the direction of the offset.

53. **Create** the Cut-Extrude3 feature based on the bottom face of the model. Utilize the Offset from Surface End Condition. Enter 5mm from the provided model information.

At this time, your model should have a mass of **14198.79** grams.

If you use faces vs. dimensions when creating features, this can help when you need to create a design change to maintain the design intent of the part.

Mass = 14198.79 grams

Volume = 1843998.20 cubic millimeters

Surface area = 243226.60 square millimeters

54. **Insert** six (6) Constant radius Fillet features (10mm) on the Cut-Extrude3 feature per the provided information.

Insert the last feature for the part - Chamfer1.

55. **Create** a Chamfer (Angle distance) feature on the internal diameter edges of the cylinders. Angle = 45. Distance = 2mm. Note: select four edges.

56. **Calculate** the Mass Properties of the model.

57. **Select 14207.34** grams for the answer in this section. The number matches the answer of d. You should be within 1% of the stated value before you move to the next section to modify the original part.

Mass properties of Part1
 Configuration: Default
 Coordinate system: -- default --

Density = 0.01 grams per cubic millimeter

Mass = 14207.34 grams

Volume = 1845108.71 cubic millimeters

Surface area = 242206.25 square millimeters

Center of mass: (millimeters)
 X = -103.57
 Y = 50.63
 Z = -111.99

58. **Save** the part.

59. **Rename** Part1 to Part2 for the second question. You are finished with this section.

-Measure the mass of the part.

What is the mass of the part (grams)?

a) 14139.65
b) 14298.56
c) 15118.41
d) 14207.34

☼ Always enter the needed decimal places in the answer field.

☼ This section presents a representation of the types of questions that you will see in this segment of the exam.

☼ At the time of this writing, there were slight variations in Mass Properties between SolidWorks 32 bit versus 64 bit. These variations are still within the 1% required for the CSWP exam segments. Always save your models to verify your results.

Segment 1 of the CSWP CORE exam - Second question

In this section, modify the original part using Global Variables. The material and units are the same but the variables A thru E are different from their original values.

The Hole Wizard feature remains the same and the equation X and Y remain the same from the original part.

Read the question carefully. This section provides a single fill in the blank format, not a multiple choice format.

Provided Information:

Update parameters of the initial part.

Unit system: MMGS (millimeter, gram, second)

Decimal places: 2

Part origin: Arbitrary

Material: Alloy Steel

Density: 0.0077 g/mm^3

All holes through all unless shown otherwise.

Use the following parameters and equations which correspond to the dimensions labeled in the images:

A = 225 mm

B = 210 mm

C = 176 mm

D = 137 mm

E = 39 mm

F = Hole Wizard Standard: ANSI Metric - Counterbore

    Type: Hex Bolt - ANSI B18.2.3.5M

    Size: M8

    Fit: Close

    Through Hole Diameter: 15.00 mm

    Counterbore Diameter: 30.00 mm

    Counterbore Depth: 10.00 mm

    End Condition: Through All

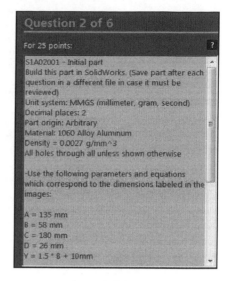

Actual CSWP
exam format

X = A/3

Y = B/3 + 10mm

Hint #1: The dimensions that are to be linked or updated and are variable will be labeled with letters. Any dimensions that are simple value changes from one stage to another will be circled in the images.

Hint #2: To save the most time, make use of linked dimensional values and equations.

Measure the mass of the part.

What is the mass of the part (grams)?

SolidWorks displays a circle, ellipse or a square around the areas and features that require modification from the original part.

This section presents a representation of the types of questions that you will see in this segment of the exam.

🔅 The images displayed on the exam are not to scale due to differences in the parts being downloaded for each tester.

🔅 Prior to SolidWorks 2013, a method commonly used to define variables for CSWP exam problems was to use Linked Values. Linked Values, also called linked dimensions, connect two or more dimensions without using equations or relations. Linked Values can still be used today in SolidWorks 2013 and SolidWorks 2014. The method to apply Linked Values is described in videos included in the book's DVD.

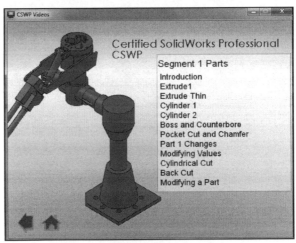

For SolidWorks 2013 and SolidWorks 2014, the method of using Global Variables to define variables for the CSWP exam problems is documented in the book. Global Variables are easier to find and change in the CSWP exam problems.

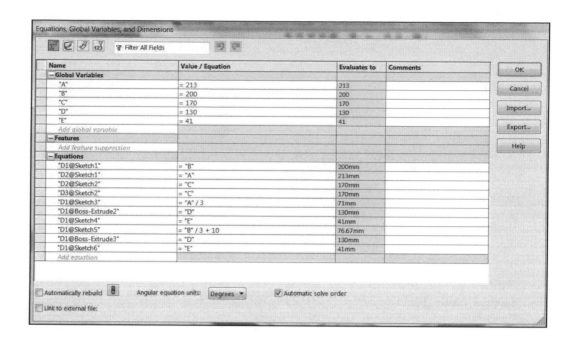

Name	Value / Equation	Evaluates to	Comments
— Global Variables			
"A"	= 213	213	
"B"	= 200	200	
"C"	= 170	170	
"D"	= 130	130	
"E"	= 41	41	
Add global variable			
— Features			
Add feature suppression			
— Equations			
"D1@Sketch1"	= "B"	200mm	
"D2@Sketch1"	= "A"	213mm	
"D2@Sketch2"	= "C"	170mm	
"D3@Sketch2"	= "C"	170mm	
"D1@Sketch3"	= "A" / 3	71mm	
"D1@Boss-Extrude2"	= "D"	130mm	
"D1@Sketch4"	= "E"	41mm	
"D1@Sketch5"	= "B" / 3 + 10	76.67mm	
"D1@Boss-Extrude3"	= "D"	130mm	
"D1@Sketch6"	= "E"	41mm	
Add equation			

SolidWorks 2014 screen shot Part 1

Let's begin.

Modify the variables that are different from Part1.

1. **Display** the Equations, Global Variables, and Dimension dialog box.

2. **Enter** the five Global Variables (A, B, C, D & E) as illustrated.

A = 213 mm	A = 225 mm
B = 200 mm	B = 210 mm
C = 170 mm	C = 176 mm
D = 130 mm	D = 137 mm
E = 41 mm	E = 39 mm

X = A/3
Y = B/3 + 10mm

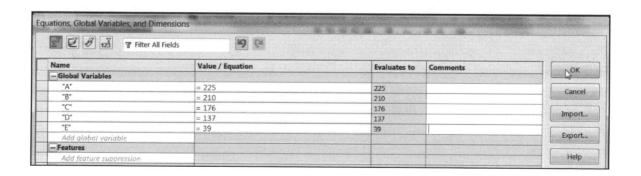

Name	Value / Equation	Evaluates to	Comments
— Global Variables			
"A"	= 225	225	
"B"	= 210	210	
"C"	= 176	176	
"D"	= 137	137	
"E"	= 39	39	
Add global variable			
— Features			
Add feature suppression			

Note you can double-click on a feature to modify the Global Variable.

3. **Calculate** the mass of the model in grams.

4. **Enter 16490.48** grams. In the CSWP exam you will need to enter this number exactly. You need to be within 1% of the stated value in the single answer format to get this question correct.

5. **Save** the part.

6. **Rename** Part2 to Part3 for the third question of the exam.

Always enter the needed decimal places (in this case 2) in the answer field.

You should have the exact answer (within 1% of the stated value in the multiple choice section) before you move on to the next question.

Segment 1 of the CSWP CORE exam - Third question

Update various parameters of the part. Modify the dimensions under Global Variables. Read the question carefully. Identify what variables and equations are the same vs. different. Has the material changed? Did a feature change? A question will be presented to you in multiple steps and you need to get each step correct to get the question correct.

Provided Information:

Update parameters of the initial part.

Unit system: MMGS (millimeter, gram, second)

Decimal places: 2

Part origin: Arbitrary

Material: Alloy Steel

Density: 0.0077 g/mm^3

All holes through all unless shown otherwise.

Use the following parameters and equations which correspond to the dimensions labeled in the images:

A = 209 mm

B = 218 mm

C = 169 mm

D = 125 mm

E = 41 mm

F = Hole Wizard Standard: ANSI Metric - Counterbore

    Type: Hex Bolt - ANSI B18.2.3.5M

    Size: M8

    Fit: Close

    Through Hole Diameter: 15.00 mm

    Counterbore Diameter: 30.00 mm

    Counterbore Depth: 10.00 mm

    End Condition: Through All

X = A/3

Y = B/3 + 10mm

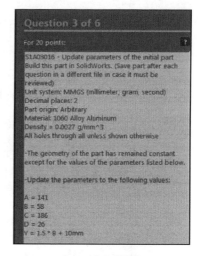

Actual CSWP
exam format

Hint #1: The dimensions that are to be linked or updated, and are variable, will be labeled with letters. Any dimensions that are simple value changes from one stage to another will be circled in the images.

Hint #2: To save the most time, make use of linked dimensional values and equations.

Measure the mass of the part.

What is the mass of the part (grams)?

To display all dimensions, right-click Annotations folder from the FeatureManager and check the Display Annotations box.

Let's begin.

1. **Display** the Equations, Global Variables, and Dimension dialog box.

2. **Enter** the five Global Variables (A, B, C, D & E) as illustrated. Modify the variables that are different.

A = 225 mm	A = 209 mm
B = 210 mm	B = 218 mm
C = 176 mm	C = 169 mm
D = 137 mm	D = 125 mm
E = 39 mm	E = 41 mm

X = A/3
Y = B/3 + 10mm

The equations (**X** = A/3, **Y** = B/3 + 10mm) have not been modified between the first, second or third question.

The CSWP exam in this section provides variables that either increase or decrease from the original part question. Design for this during the exam.

3. **Calculate** the mass of the model in grams.

4. **Enter 15100.47** grams.

5. **Save** the part.

6. **Rename** Part3 to Part4 for the fourth question of the exam.

Always enter the needed decimal places (in this case 2) in the answer field.

You should have the exact answer (within 1% of the stated value in the multiple choice section) before you move on to the next question.

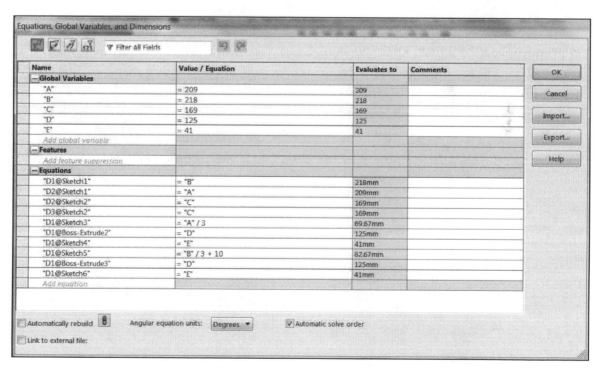

Name	Value / Equation	Evaluates to	Comments
Global Variables			
"A"	= 209	209	
"B"	= 218	218	
"C"	= 169	169	
"D"	= 125	125	
"E"	= 41	41	
Add global variable			
Features			
Add feature suppression			
Equations			
"D1@Sketch1"	= "B"	218mm	
"D2@Sketch1"	= "A"	209mm	
"D2@Sketch2"	= "C"	169mm	
"D3@Sketch2"	= "C"	169mm	
"D1@Sketch3"	= "A" / 3	69.67mm	
"D1@Boss-Extrude2"	= "D"	125mm	
"D1@Sketch4"	= "E"	41mm	
"D1@Sketch5"	= "B" / 3 + 10	82.67mm	
"D1@Boss-Extrude3"	= "D"	125mm	
"D1@Sketch6"	= "E"	41mm	
Add equation			

Segment 1 of the CSWP CORE exam - Fourth question

Stage 2: Modify the part using the following dimensions (These images are to be used to answer questions 4 and 5).

Note: The changes from the initial part are concentrated in areas AA, BB and CC shown in the first two images.

The needed modifications AA, BB, and CC are displayed with a circle, ellipse or a square in the CSWP exam. Compare the information with your existing part. This question provides a multiple choice answer.

Actual CSWP
exam format

Provided Information:

4. Stage 2

Unit system: MMGS (millimeter, gram, second)

Decimal places: 2

Part origin: Arbitrary

Material: Alloy Steel

Density: 0.0077 g/mm^3

All holes through all unless shown otherwise.

Use the following parameters and equations which correspond to the dimensions labeled in the images:

A = 221 mm

B = 211 mm

C = 165 mm

D = 121 mm

E = 37 mm

X = A/3

Y = B/3 + 15mm

Note: The equation for Y has changed from the initial part.

Hint #1: The dimensions that are to be linked or updated, and are variable, will be labeled with letters. Any dimensions that are simple value changes from one stage to another will be circled in the images.

Hint #2: To save the most time, make use of linked dimensional values and equations.

Measure the mass of the part.

What is the mass of the part (grams)?

a) 13095.40

b) 13206.40

c) 13313.35

d) 13395.79

The material and units are the same. Equation Λ is the same. Variables A thru E are different. The Hole Wizard feature is removed with a few other features as illustrated. Equation Y is different. Read the question carefully.

Address AA modification in the model. Create a single pocket and remove the Hole Wizard feature along with the Boss-Extrude4 feature and a few fillets. Recover and repair from missing items.

Let's begin.

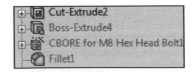

1. **Suppress** Fillet1, CBORE and Boss-Extrrude4. A dialog box is displayed.

2. **Press** the Stop and Repair button from the SolidWorks dialog box. Fillet3 has a reference issue. There are missing items in the existing feature.

⚡ As a general rule, suppress features before you delete them. This will inform you if there are any rebuild or feature errors during modification in the exam.

3. **Edit** the Fillet3 feature and repair. Delete any missing edges and insert the new edge.

But wait, you can't insert the new edge (as illustrated) because it is part of the offset from the original sketch when you created the part.

Create a square corner for Sketch10 to select the needed edge for Fillet3.

4. **Edit** Sketch10 from the Cut-Extrude3 feature. Delete the fillet.

5. **Insert** the needed edge for Fillet3 using the Trim Entities sketch tool (Corner option).

6. **Edit** the Fillet3 feature and add the needed edge that you just created. Verify that you have 5 fillets with the radius of 10mm. There are no errors displayed in the FeatureManager.

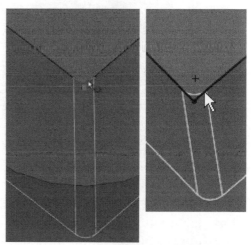

7. **Delete** all suppressed features and any unneeded sketch in the FeatureManager: Fillet1, CBORE, Boss-Extrude4 and Sketch7. Suppress features before you delete them. This will inform you if there are any rebuild or feature errors during modification in the exam.

8. **Roll** back the Rollback bar in the FeatureManager.

9. **Calculate** the mass of the model in grams.

Mass properties of Part4
    Configuration: Default
    Coordinate system: -- default --

Density = 0.01 grams per cubic millimeter

Mass = 14378.42 grams

Volume = 1867327.21 cubic millimeters

Surface area = 243380.56 square millimeters

Center of mass: (millimeters)
    X = -108.57
    Y = 51.67
    Z = -116.51

10. Your mass at this time should be **14378.42 grams**.

You should have the exact answer (within 1% of the stated value in the multiple choice section) before you move on to the next question.

11. **Save** the part.

Address the BB modification in the model. Create a circular cut as illustrated on the left cylinder. The circular cut is offset 30mm from the front face of the cylinder. The depth of the cut is 30mm.

From the front view, the circular cut is offset 10mm and the circular cut does not go completely through the Extrude-Thin1 feature.

Last, modify the Chamfer feature of the cylinders.

In this section utilize the Offset Entities, Convert Entities, Line and Trim Sketch tools to create the Base Sketch for the Extruded Cut feature.

Let's begin.

12. **Create** a Sketch plane (30mm) offset from the front face of the cylinder as illustrated. Plane3 is displayed in the FeatureManager.

13. **Create** the Base Sketch on Plane3. Apply the Convert Entities Sketch tool to utilize the outside cylindrical geometry of the tube.

14. **Apply** the Offset Entities Sketch tool with an offset distance of 10mm. Click the outside cylindrical edge and reverse the direction if needed. You created an inside and outside ring for the Extruded Cut feature on your Base Sketch (Sketch11).

15. **Create** two vertical lines from the outside cylindrical edge to the inside cylindrical edge of the ring. The sketch is fully defined.

16. **Trim** any unwanted sketch geometry to finish the sketch for the Extruded Cut feature. Your Base sketch should consist of two arcs and two vertical lines.

17. **Create** an Extruded Cut feature with a depth of 30mm. The Extruded Cut feature removes the needed material and keeps the Extrude-Thin1 feature unbroken.

Next, address the modification of the Chamfer feature in the front face of the cylinder.

18. **Modify** the cylinder Chamfer feature from 45 degrees to 30 degrees.

At this time your model should have a mass of **13983.95 grams**.

19. **Save** the part.

Always enter the needed decimal places (in this case 2) in the answer field.

Mass properties of Part4A
    Configuration: Default
    Coordinate system: -- default --

Density = 0.01 grams per cubic millimeter

Mass = 13983.95 grams

Volume = 1816096.79 cubic millimeters

⊞ Boss-Extrude1
⊞ Extrude-Thin1
   Plane1
⊞ Boss-Extrude2
⊞ Cut-Extrude1
   Plane2
⊞ Boss-Extrude3
⊞ Cut-Extrude2
   Fillet2
⊞ Cut-Extrude3
   Fillet3
   Chamfer1
   Plane3
⊞ Cut-Extrude4

Address the Extruded Cut and fillet feature and then address the Global Variables A thru E and equation Y.

There are numerous ways to create the sketch for the Extruded Cut feature. In this case, utilize Construction geometry. Construction geometry helps you create a sketch but is not part of the feature.

View the DVD for an alternative method using the Rollback bar and existing geometry to create the sketch for the Extruded Cut feature.

20. **Create** a sketch using the Offset Entities Sketch tool on the top back face. Enter 9mm for Offset distance. Reverse the direction if needed.

21. **Window-select** the part. Check the For construction box. Again, construction geometry helps create a sketch but is not part of the feature.

Create a 90^0 Arc and inference the vertical line from the Extrude-Thin1 feature.

22. **Create** a 90^0 Arc. Use the Centerpoint Arc Sketch tool. Click the centerpoint as illustrated, drag directly to the right until you see the inference symbol on the construction arc. Click the start point. Drag downward and click the end point to create the 90^0 Arc. Note the mouse pointer displays A = 90 for angle feedback.

Sometimes when you convert sketch geometry, unwanted arcs and points are created. In the next section, delete any unwanted sketch geometry to cleanly create Sketch12.

23. **Remove** the top left fillet with the Trim Entities Sketch tool.

24. **Restore** the corner of the fillet feature with the Trim Entities Sketch tool (Corner option) or by just dragging the endpoints together.

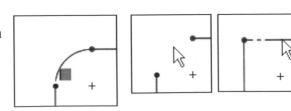

25. **Remove** all unwanted sketch geometry around the start point of the 90^0 Arc.

26. **Remove** all unwanted sketch geometry around the end point of the 90^0 Arc.

Now you can utilize the horizontal and vertical construction geometry with the 9mm offset with new lines and the Arc is created correctly. Again there are other ways to create the sketch for the Extruded Cut feature.

27. **Complete** the close sketch profile with the Line Sketch tool.

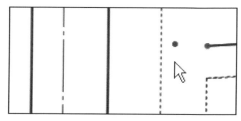

Insert all needed Geometric relations.

28. **Insert** a vertical relation between the end point of the Arc and the corner point of the Thin-Extrude1 feature. The sketch should be fully defined and displayed in black.

29. **Create** the Extruded Cut feature. Apply the Up To Surface End Condition and click the inside face of Cut-Extrude3. The two surfaces provide a similar dimension.

30. **Apply** the Fillet feature. Insert three fillets per the provided drawing. 10mm is the fillet radius.

At this time your model should have a mass of **12154.09 grams**.

31. **Display** the Equations, Global Variables and Dimension dialog box.

32. **Enter** the five new Global Variables (A, B, C, D & E) and the new Y equation as illustrated.

A = 221 mm
B = 211 mm
C = 165 mm
D = 121 mm
E = 37 mm
X = A/3
Y = B/3 + 15mm

Note: The equation for Y has changed from the initial part.

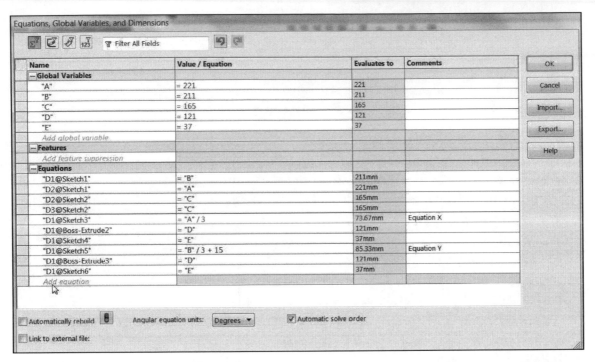

33. **Calculate** the mass of the model.

34. **Select 13206.40 grams**. The number matches the answer of b. You should be within 1% of the stated value before you move to the next section to modify the part.

35. **Save** the part.

36. **Rename** Part4 to Part5.

Always save your models to verify your results.

Use the Comments box to label your equations.

Confirm that your math is correct. Use the Measure tool during the exam.

Mass properties of Part5
   Configuration: Default
   Coordinate system: -- default --

Density = 0.01 grams per cubic millimeter

Mass = 13206.40 grams

Volume = 1715116.48 cubic millimeters

Surface area = 253729.21 square millimeters

Center of mass: (millimeters)
   X = -97.24
   Y = 57.94
   Z = -114.16

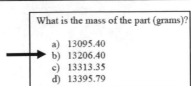

What is the mass of the part (grams)?

   a) 13095.40
   b) 13206.40
   c) 13313.35
   d) 13395.79

Segment 1 of the CSWP CORE exam - Fifth question

Compare the provided information with your existing part. The Global Variables A thru E change, and the equations are the same from the last question but equation Y has changed from the initial part. This question provides a fill in the blank format.

Provided Information:

5. Stage 2 - Update Parameters

Unit system: MMGS (millimeter, gram, second)

Decimal places: 2

Part origin: Arbitrary

Material: Alloy Steel

Density: 0.0077 g/mm^3

All holes through all unless shown otherwise.

Use the following parameters and equations which correspond to the dimensions labeled in the images:

A = 229 mm

B = 217 mm

C = 163 mm

D = 119 mm

E = 34 mm

X = A/3

Y = B/3 + 15mm

Hint #1: The dimensions that are to be linked or updated and are variable will be labeled with letters. Any dimensions that are simple value changes from one stage to another will be circled in the images.

Hint #2: To save the most time, make use of linked dimensional values and equations.

Measure the mass of the part.

What is the mass of the part (grams)?

Let's begin.

1. **Display** the Equations, Global Variables and Dimension dialog box.

2. **Enter** the five new Global Variables (A, B, C, D & E) as illustrated.

$$A = 229 \text{ mm}$$
$$B = 217 \text{ mm}$$
$$C = 163 \text{ mm}$$
$$D = 119 \text{ mm}$$
$$E = 34 \text{ mm}$$
$$X = A/3$$
$$Y = B/3 + 15\text{mm}$$

3. **Calculate** the mass of the part.

4. **Enter 14208.01 grams**.

5. **Save** the part.

At the end of the exam, view the Summary dialog box. Press the End Examination button only if you are finished.

☀ Always enter the needed decimal places in the answer field.

☀ The sample CSWP exam only covers segment 1. Time yourself on the practice exam. You should be able to finish the sample Segment 1 CSWP CORE exam in approximately 60 - 75 minutes.

Actual CSWP exam format

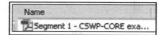

☀ Prior to SolidWorks 2013, a method commonly used to define variables for CSWP exam problems was to use Linked Values. Linked Values, also called linked dimensions, connect two or more dimensions without using equations or relations. Linked Values can still be used today in SolidWorks 2013 and SolidWorks 2014. The method to apply Linked Values is described in videos included in the book's DVD.

When you pass the first segment of the CSWP CORE exam you will receive the following email. Click on the SolidWorks Certification Center hyperlink to login, activate and view your certificate.

Congratulations David!
You have been issued a certificate in SolidWorks® Virtual Test Center indicating that you have successfully completed the requirements for **Segment 1 of Certified SolidWorks Professional Core.**

CertificateID:

Visit your certificate area on SolidWorks® Certification Center. Click My Account to access your certificates and exams.

Congratulations,
Avelino Rochino

SolidWorks® is a registered trademark of Dassault Systèmes SolidWorks Corp.

Use the SolidWorks Tutorials and SolidWorks Help to find additional information on Global Variables and equations before the exam. A novice using help files during the exam will not have enough time.

For many features in SolidWorks 2013 and newer (Extruded Boss/Base, Extruded Cut, Simple Hole, Revolved Boss/Base, Revolved Cut, Fillet, Chamfer, Scale, Shell, Rib, Circular Pattern, Linear Pattern, Curve Driven Pattern, Revolved Surface, Extruded Surface, Fillet Surface, Edge Flange and Base Flange) you can enter and modify equations directly in the PropertyManager fields that allow numerical inputs.

You can create equations with global variables, functions, and file properties without accessing the Equations, Global Variables and Dimensions dialog box.

For example, in the PropertyManager for the Extruded Boss/Base feature, you can enter equations in:

- Depth fields for Direction 1 and Direction 2

- Draft fields for Direction 1 and Direction 2

- Thickness fields for a Thin Feature with two direction types

- Offset Distance field

To create an equation in a numeric input field, start by entering = (equal sign). A drop-down list displays options for global variables, functions, and file properties. Numeric input fields that contain equations can display either the equation itself or its evaluated value.

You can toggle between the equation and the value by clicking the Equations or Global Variable button that appears at the beginning of the field.

In SolidWorks 2013 and newer, right-click anywhere on an extruded feature and change the end condition from the shortcut menu. Click in empty space, on geometry, or on the handle. The shortcut menu provides all the options for Direction 1 and Direction 2. Note: Options are document dependent.

Segment 1 of the CSWP CORE exam - Additional Practice Problems

In this section, there are fewer step-by-step procedures. Use the provided initial and final models and drawings on the DVD with the rollback bar if needed.

Question 1:
Build the following part in SolidWorks.

Provided information:

Units: MMGS (millimeter, gram, second)

Decimal Places: 2

Part Origin: Arbitrary

Material: 6061 Alloy

Density: 2700 kg/m^2

All holes through all unless shown otherwise.

Use the following parameters and equations which correspond to the dimensions labeled in the images:

A: 60 mm

B: 45 mm

C: 52 degrees

D: 20 mm

X: 175 + D/2

What is the mass of the part in (grams)?

a) 686.50

b) 1858.61

c) 1845.10

d) 1742.88

You should have the exact answer (within 1% of the stated value in the multiple choice section) before you move on to the next question.

🔆 There are numerous ways to build the model in this section. A goal is to display different design intents and techniques.

Let's begin.

Create a New part in SolidWorks.

1. **Create** a folder to save your models.

2. **Create** a new part.

3. **Set** document properties (drafting standard, units and precision) for the model.

4. **Assign** 6061 Alloy material.

In this problem, first address Global Variables and Equations.

5. **Click** Tools, Equations. The Equations, Global Variables, and Dimensions dialog box is displayed.

6. **Enter** the below information for the provided parameters and equations as illustrated.

7. **Click** OK from the dialog box.

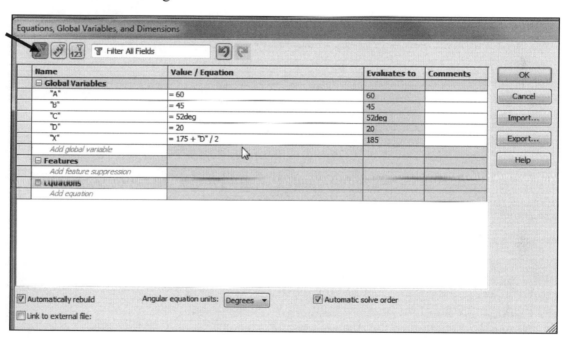

8. **Expand** the Equations folder in the FeatureManager. View the results.

SolidWorks 2013 provides the ability to select units from a drop down menu in the Value / Equation column.

Start the Base feature (Boss-Extrude1) with Sketch1.

9. **Create** Sketch1. Select the Front plane and utilize Global Variables as illustrated.

10. **Create** Boss-Extrude1. Apply the Mid-Plane End Condition with a distance of 20mm. Link the extruded distance to the Global Variable D. At this time your mass is 614.36 grams.

11. **Create** Sketch2 on the Front plane for the Revolve1 feature. Note the geometric relations in the sketch. There are small line segments in this sketch. Zoom in to select correct references.

12. **Utilize** Global Variables. Note: There are many different ways to create this model.

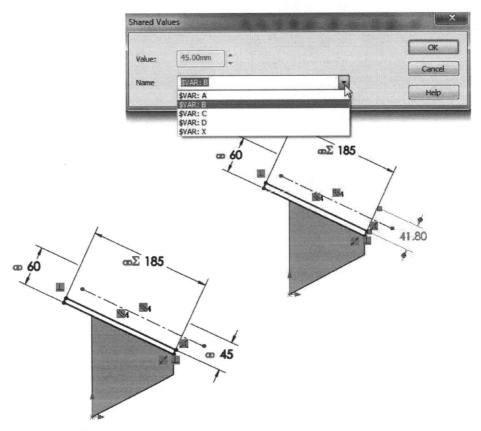

The CSWP exam in this section provides variables that either increase or decrease from the original part question. Design for this during the exam.

13. **Create** Revolve1. Revolve1 is the top tube feature as illustrated. At this time your model should have a mass of **1232.24 grams**.

Merge the two bodies.

14. **Create** Sketch3. Select the top face of Boss-Extrude1. Utilize the Convert entities Sketch tool.

15. **Create** Boss-Extrude2. Extrude Up to Next (End Condition) making a single (Merge results) body part. At this time your model should have a mass of **1236.45 grams**.

Always enter the needed decimal places (in this case 2) in the answer field.

Confirm that your math is correct. Use the Measure tool during the exam.

16. **Save** the part.

17. **Name** the part CSWP PP2-1.

Mass properties of Part1
Configuration: Default
Coordinate system: --default--

Density = 0.00 grams per cubic millimeter

Mass = 1236.45 grams

Volume = 457943.65 cubic millimeters

Boss-Extrude

From
Sketch Plane

Direction 1
Up To Next

☑ Merge result

☐ Draft outward

CSWP PP2-1 (Default<<Default
- Sensors
- Annotations
- Equations
- 6061 Alloy
- Front Plane
- Top Plane
- Right Plane
- Origin
- Boss-Extrude1
  - Sketch1
- Revolve1
  - Sketch2
- Boss-Extrude2
  - Sketch3

Create the bottom tube with a second
Revolve feature.

18. **Create** Sketch4 on the Front plane for
the Revolve2 feature. Note the
geometric relations in the sketch. There
are small line segments in this sketch.
Zoom in to select correct references.
Insert all needed relations and
dimensions.

19. **Create** Revolve2. Revolve2 is the bottom tube
feature as illustrated. At this time your model
should have a mass
of **1854.33 grams.**

Mass = 1854.33 grams

Volume = 686789.04 cubic millimeters

Surface area = 153882.29 square millimeters

Center of mass: (millimeters)
X = 52.91
Y = 77.44
Z = 0.00

Merge the two bodies.

20. **Create** Sketch5. Select the bottom face of Boss-Extrude1. Utilize the Convert Entities Sketch tool.

21. **Create** Boss-Extrude3. Extrude Up to Next (End Condition) making a single (Merge results) body part.

22. **Calculate** the mass of the model in grams.

23. **Enter 1858.61** grams. In the CSWP exam you will need to enter this number exactly. You need to be within 1% of the stated value in the single answer format to get this question correct.

24. **Save** the part.

25. **Rename** the CSWP PP2-1 part to CSWP PP2-2.

What is the mass of the part in (grams)?
a) 686.50

b) 1858.61

c) 1845.10

d) 1742.88

Mass properties of CSWP PP2-1
  Configuration: Default
  Coordinate system: -- default --

Density = 0.00 grams per cubic millimeter

Mass = 1858.61 grams

Volume = 688375.17 cubic millimeters

Surface area = 148719.04 square millimeters

Center of mass: (millimeters)
  X = 52.93
  Y = 77.34
  Z = 0.00

CSWP PP2-1 (Default<<Defaul
  Sensors
  Annotations
  Equations
    "A"=60
    "B"=45
    "C"=52deg
    "D"=20
    "X"=185
  6061 Alloy
  Front Plane
  Top Plane
  Right Plane
  Origin
  Boss-Extrude1
    Sketch1
  Revolve1
    Sketch2
  Boss-Extrude2
    Sketch3
  Revolve2
    Sketch4
  Boss-Extrude3
    Sketch5

☀ This section presents a representation of the types of questions that you will see in this segment of the exam.

☀ At the time of this writing, there were slight variations in Mass Properties between SolidWorks 32 bit versus 64 bit. These variations are still within the 1% required for the CSWP exam segments. Always save your models to verify your results.

Question 1: Part II

Compare the provided information (dimensions, material, variables and equation) with the existing part (CSWP PP2-2) which you created in the previous section. Use the provided initial and final models and drawings on the DVD with the rollback bar if needed.

What is the mass of the part in grams?

Provided information:

Units: MMGS (millimeter, gram, second)

Decimal Places: 2

Part Origin: Arbitrary

Material: 6061 Alloy

Density: 2700 kg/m^2

All holes through all unless shown otherwise.

Use the following parameters and equations which correspond to the dimensions labeled in the images.

A: 80 mm

B: 60 mm

C: 50 degree

D: 40 mm

X: 180 + D/2

You should have the exact answer (within 1% of the stated value in the multiple choice section) before you move on to the next question.

There are numerous ways to build the model in this section. A goal is to display different design intents and techniques.

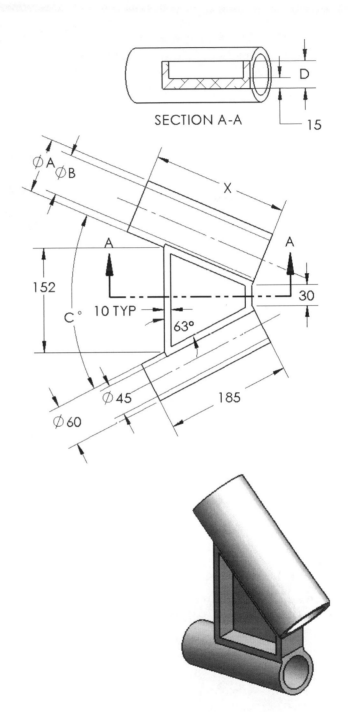

Let's begin.

Compare the provided **dimensions**, **materials**, **variables** and **equation**.

Question 1:	**Question 1: Part II**
Build the following part in SolidWorks.	Compare the provided information (dimensions, material, variables and equation) with the existing part (CSWP PP2-2) which you created in the previous section. Use the provided initial and final models and drawings on the DVD with the rollback bar if needed.
Provided information:	
Units: MMGS (millimeter, gram, second)	
Decimal Places: 2	
Part Origin: Arbitrary	What is the mass of the part in grams?
Material: 6061 Alloy	Provided information:
Density: 2700 kg/m^2	**Units**: MMGS (millimeter, gram, second)
All holes through all unless shown otherwise.	**Decimal Places**: 2
Use the following parameters and equations which correspond to the dimensions labeled in the images:	**Part Origin**: Arbitrary
A: 60 mm	**Material**: 6061 Alloy
B: 45 mm	**Density**: 2700 kg/m^2
C: 52 degrees	All holes through all unless shown otherwise.
D: 20 mm	Use the following parameters and equations which correspond to the dimensions labeled in the images.
X: 175 + D/2	**A**: 80 mm
What is the mass of the part in (grams)?	**B**: 60 mm
a) 686.50	**C**: 50
b) 1858.61	**D**: 40 mm
c) 1845.10	**X**: 180 + D/2
d) 1742.88	

Where do you start? Three variables and the equation were changed. Edit the Equations, Global Variables, and Dimensions dialog box.

A: 60 mm	**A**: 80 mm
B: 45 mm	**B**: 60 mm
C: 52 degrees	**C**: 50 degree
D: 20 mm	**D**: 40 mm
X: 175 + D/2	**X**: 180 + D/2

1. **Right-click** the Equations folder. Click Manager Equations. The Equations, Global Variables, and Dimensions dialog box is displayed.

2. **Enter** the below information for the provided parameters and equation as illustrated.

3. **Click** OK from the dialog box.

At this time your model should have a mass of **3153.76 grams**.

4. **Expand** the Equations folder. View the results.

Address the Offset Extruded Cut feature displayed in the illustration.

5. **Create** Sketch6 on the front face of the plate. Utilize the Offset Entities Sketch tool. Enter 10mm depth to the inside.

6. **Display** an Isometric view to create the Extruded Cut feature.

7. **Create** Cut-Extrude1. Utilize the Offset from Surface End Condition. Select the back face. Enter 15mm (Depth) as illustrated.

8. **Save** the part.

9. **Calculate** the mass of the model in grams.

What is the mass of the part in grams? Check your work.

10. **Enter 2531.70 grams**.

11. **Rename** part CSWP PP2-2 to CSWP PP2-3.

Mass properties of CSWP PP2-3
   Configuration: Default
   Coordinate system: -- default --

Density = 0.00 grams per cubic millimeter

Mass = 2531.70 grams

Volume = 937665.51 cubic millimeters

Surface area = 188918.31 square millimeters

Center of mass: (millimeters)
   X = 54.68
   Y = 102.84
   Z = -1.84

SECTION A-A

Question 1: Part III

Build the following part in SolidWorks.

Compare the provided information (dimensions, material, variables and equation) with the existing part (CSWP PP2-3) which you created in the previous section.

What is the mass of the part in grams?

Provided Information:

Units: MMGS (millimeter, gram, second)

Decimal Places: 2

Part Origin: Arbitrary

Material: 6061 Alloy

Density: 2700 kg/m^2

All holes through all unless shown otherwise.

Use the following parameters and equations which correspond to the dimensions labeled in the images.

A: 80 mm

B: 60 mm

C: 50 degrees

D: 40 mm

X: 180 + D/2

SECTION A-A

DETAIL B

Let's begin.

Compare the **dimensions**, **material**, **variables** and **equation**.

Question 1: Part II	Question 1: Part III
Compare the provided information (dimensions, material, variables and equation) with the existing part (CSWP PP2-2) which you created in the previous section. Use the provided initial and final models and drawings on the DVD with the rollback bar if needed.	Build the following part in SolidWorks. Compare the provided information (dimensions, material, variables and equation) with the existing part (CSWP PP2-3) which you created in the previous section.
What is the mass of the part in grams?	What is the mass of the part in grams?
Provided information:	Provided Information:
Units: MMGS (millimeter, gram, second)	**Units**: MMGS (millimeter, gram, second)
Decimal Places: 2	**Decimal Places**: 2
Part Origin: Arbitrary	**Part Origin**: Arbitrary
Material: 6061 Alloy	**Material**: 6061 Alloy
Density: 2700 kg/m^2	**Density**: 2700 kg/m^2
All holes through all unless shown otherwise.	All holes through all unless shown otherwise.
Use the following parameters and equations which correspond to the dimensions labeled in the images.	Use the following parameters and equations which correspond to the dimensions labeled in the images.
A: 80 mm	**A**: 80 mm
B: 60 mm	**B**: 60 mm
C: 50	**C**: 50
D: 40 mm	**D**: 40 mm
X: 180 + D/2	**X**: 180 + D/2

None of the variables or equation were modified between the second and third question. Start with the first Boss-Extrude1 feature.

A: 80 mm	A: 80 mm
B: 60 mm	B: 60 mm
C: 50 degree	C: 50 degree
D: 40 mm	D: 40 mm
X: 180 + D/2	X: 180 + D/2

1. **Drag** the rollback bar directly under Boss-Extrude1.

2. **Edit** the base sketch (Sketch1) according to the Detail view. Create a 30mm x 60mm corner rectangle. Trim geometry.

Original Base Sketch

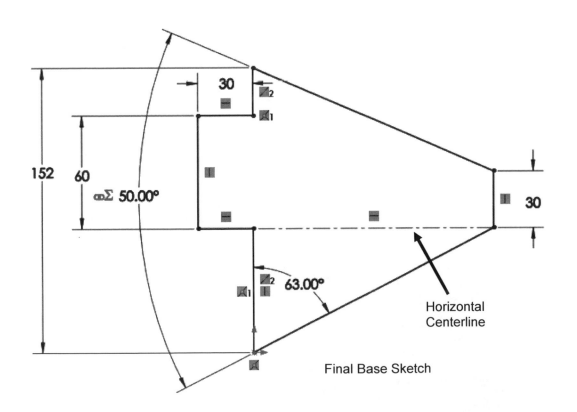

Final Base Sketch

3. **Save** the part.

4. **Calculate** the mass of the model in grams.

What is the mass of the part in grams?

5. Enter **2645.10 grams**.

Mass properties of CSWP PP2-3
   Configuration: Default
   Coordinate system: -- default --

Density = 0.00 grams per cubic millimeter

Mass = 2645.10 grams

Volume = 979665.51 cubic millimeters

Surface area = 196418.31 square millimeters

Center of mass: (millimeters)
   X = 51.39
   Y = 102.57
   Z = -1.99

☀ Always enter the needed decimal places in the answer field.

You are finished with this section. Good luck on the exam in Segment 1.

☀ At the time of this writing, there were slight variations in Mass Properties between SolidWorks 32 bit versus 64 bit. These variations are still within the 1% required for the CSWP exam segments. Always save your models to verify your results.

CSWP PP2-3 (Default<<Default
- Sensors
- Annotations
- Equations
- 6061 Alloy
- Front Plane
- Top Plane
- Right Plane
- Origin
- Boss-Extrude1
  - Sketch1
- Revolve1
  - Sketch2
- Boss-Extrude2
  - Sketch3
- Revolve2
  - Sketch4
- Boss-Extrude3
  - Sketch5
- Cut-Extrude1
  - Sketch6

🔆 SolidWorks displays a circle, ellipse or a square around the areas and features that requires modification from the original part.

🔆 This section presents a representation of the types of questions that you will see in this segment of the exam.

🔆 The images displayed on the exam are not to scale due to differences in the parts being downloaded for each tester.

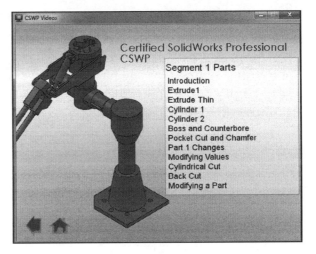

Below are former screen shots from a previous CSWP exam in Segment 1.

CHAPTER 2 - SEGMENT 2 OF THE CORE CSWP EXAM

Introduction

The second segment of the CSWP exam is 40 minutes with nine (9) questions (11 total but two are instructional pages) divided into two categories.

The format is either multiple choice or single answer. The first question in this segment is typically in a multiple choice format.

This section presents a representation of the types of questions that you will see in this segment of the exam.

First Category:

- Creating configurations from other configurations

- Modifying configurations using a design table

- Obtaining Mass Properties of various modified configurations

Second Category:

- Modifying features and sketches of an existing part

- Recovering from rebuild errors while maintaining the overall design intent

Actual CSWP
exam format

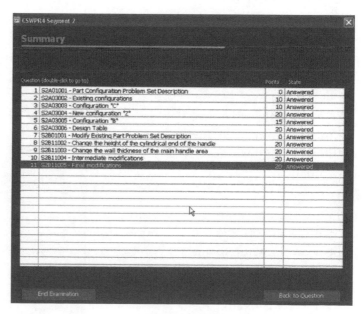

Actual CSWP
exam format

You should have the exact answer (within 1% of the stated value in the multiple choice section) before you move on to the next question. If you don't have the exact answer of the first question, you will most likely fail the following question. This is crucial as there is no partial credit.

A total score of 115 out of 155 or better is required to pass the second segment. When you pass the second segment of the CSWP CORE exam you will receive the following email.

You will be tested on data found in the Mass Properties section of SolidWorks. It is important to be familiar with accessing Mass Properties and interpreting them correctly.

SolidWorks will not accept a comma in the answer field. Only use decimal points.

Use the SolidWorks Tutorials and SolidWorks Help to find additional information on configurations and design tables before the exam. The exam is 40 minutes, a novice using help files will not obtain a passing score. This segment shows whether a user is capable of modifying basic features and getting needed data without wasting a lot of time.

If you fail a segment of the exam, you need to wait 14 days until you can retake that same segment. In that time, you can take another segment.

The purpose of this book is not to educate a new or intermediate user on SolidWorks, but to inform you on the types of questions, layout and what to expect when taking the segment portions of the CSWP CORE exam.

The images displayed on the exam are not to scale due to differences in the parts being downloaded for each tester.

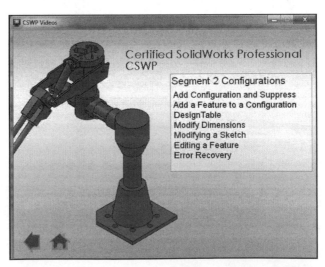

Utilize the segment videos and model folders provided in the book to follow along while using the book. Each segment video provides valuable information to successfully pass the CSWP CORE exam.

Segment 2 of the CSWP CORE Exam

Load the Testing client and read the instructions. Create a folder to save your working models. Question 1 is an instructional page.

Question 2 prompts you to click a link which will download the needed file. Download the file in your created folder for the exam.

Copy the CSWP Folder from the DVD to your hard drive. Open the Sample6 part from the Segment 2 Initial folder. This will be your downloaded part for this segment.

In this section:

- Create configurations from other configurations
- Modify configurations using a design table
- Obtain Mass Properties of various modified configurations

Let's begin.

Open the SolidWorks part. A question in this section could be - determine how many existing configurations there are in the part.

1. **Create** a folder to save your working model.

2. **Open** the Sample6 part from the Segment 2 Initial folder.

Actual CSWP exam format

3. **Click** the ConfigurationManager tab in the design tree to view the different configurations of the part.

4. **Select** 3 for the number of configurations in the multiple-choice answer section of the exam. The first question in this segment is typically in a multiple choice format.

5. **Double-click** on each configuration in the ConfigurationManager. The FeatureManager displays a different material for each configuration.

It is important that you understand that these materials will change in the exam and to understand where you would start a new configuration to the existing ConfigurationManager.

A question in this section could be - create a new configuration (sample6-4) from the existing sample6-3 configuration.

Calculate the mass of the new configuration (sample6-4) in grams. **Decimal places**: 2.

Let's begin.

6. **Double-click** sample6-3. Sample6-3 is the active Configuration.

7. **Add** a new configuration sample6-4. Sample6-4 is the current configuration.

8. **Calculate** the mass of the new configuration sample6-4 in grams.

9. **Enter 4982.03** grams for the answer. It is very important to input the proper decimal places as requested in the exam. In this case (2) two.

10. **Save** the model.

A question in this section could be - suppress a feature in some but not all configurations.

Suppress the front cut (Cut-Extrude3) and back cut (Cut-Extrude5) in the sample6-4 configuration.

Note: The Cut-Extrude3 feature references the Fillet3, Cut-Extrude5, and Fillet4 feature in the provided model.

Calculate the mass of the part in grams.

Let's begin.

There are numerous ways to address the models in this segment. A goal is to display different design intents and techniques.

11. **Suppress** the features as illustrated in the sample6-4 configuration.

12. **Calculate** the Mass Properties of configuration sample6-4 with the suppressed features.

13. **Enter 6423.17** grams for the answer. You need to be within 1% of the stated value in the single answer format to get this question correct. It is also very important to input the proper decimal places as requested in the exam. In this case there are (2) two. Round your answers if needed.

14. **Save** the part.

Mass = 6423.17 grams

Volume = 2378951.02 cubic millimeters

Surface area = 241447.39 square millimeters

A question in this section could be - create configuration sample6-5 from configuration sample6-1.

Provided Information:

Add a 30x30x10mm square in the *front left corner* of (Boss-Extrude1). Utilize the existing fillet radius as the Base Extrude1 feature in your sketch.

Calculate the mass of the part in grams.

Decimal places: 2.

Let's begin.

15. **Double-click** the sample6-1 configuration from the ConfigurationManager. Sample6-1 is the active configuration.

16. **Add** a new configuration sample6-5. Sample6-5 is the current configuration.

Create the sketch for the 30x30x10mm square. Control the sketch with geometric relations and dimensions. Do not select the midpoint of the horizontal line segment.

 Utilize the split bar to work between the FeatureManager and the ConfigurationManager.

17. **Create** the sketch (Sketch15) using the Corner Rectangle Sketch tool. Insert the needed gemoetric relation and dimension. Do not select the midpoint of the horizontal line segment.

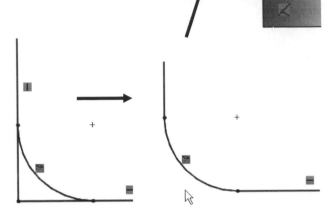

Remember it stated in the question - utilize the existing fillet radius as the Base Extrude1 feature in your sketch.

18. **Utilize** the Convert Entities Sketch tool along with the Trim Entitles Sketch tool to complete the sketch.

19. **Create** the Boss-Extrude feature with a depth of 10mm. Boss-Extrude4 is displayed in the FeatureManager.

20. **Calculate** the Mass Properties of configuration sample6-5 with the new feature.

21. **Enter 16500.44** grams for the anwser. It is very important to input the proper decimal places as requested in the exam.

Mass properties of Sample6 (Part Configuration - sample6-5)

Output coordinate System: -- default --

Density = 0.0089 grams per cubic millimeter

Mass = 16500.4393 grams

Volume = 1853981.9476 cubic millimeters

Surface area = 260946.0832 square millimeters

Center of mass: (millimeters)
  X = -98.3083
  Y = 58.4182
  Z = -113.2841

22. **Save** the part.

☀ Utilize the segment videos and model folders provided in the book to follow along while using the book. Each segment video provides valuable information to successfully pass the CSWP CORE exam.

A question in this section could be - create a new configuration sample6-6 from configuration sample6-2 in a design table by copying / pasting a new row.

Start with configuration sample6-2.

Create a design table.

Create a new configuration sample6-6 from configuration sample6-2 in the design table by copying / pasting a new row.

Change the following parameters in the design table for configuration sample6-6 to the following specified values:

- D1@Boss-Extrude1 = 35

- A@Sketch1 = 230

- B@Sketch1 = 225

Calculate the mass of the part in grams.

Decimal places: 2.

Actual CSWP
exam format

For these tasks, review the videos on the DVD that correspond to the competencies you need to know for Segment 2 of the CSWP CORE exam.

Let's begin.

1. **Double-click** sample6-2. Sample6-2 is the active configuration.

2. **Create** a design table. Use the Auto-create option.

3. **Create** a new configuration sample6-6 (copy/paste) from sample6-2 in the design table.

Check your new configuration in the ConfigurationManager. Update the design table.

4. **Exit** the design table and view the new configuration sample6-6 in the ConfigurationManager.

5. **Double-click** sample6-6. Sample6-6 is the active configuration.

6. **Edit** the design table. Do not add any columns and rows to the table at this time. View the updated design table.

Change the D1@Boss-Extrude1 = 35 parameter in the design table for configuration sample6-6.

7. **Double-click** on the Boss-Extrude1 feature. The column for the state of Boss-Extrude1 is displayed in the design table.

8. **Click** the depth dimension 25 in the Graphics window. 25 is displayed in the design table. 25 is the depth dimension for all configurations.

9. **Enter** 35 for depth dimension for configuration sample6-6.

10. **Exit** the design table. Configuration sample6-6 has a height of 35mm.

11. **Apply** the Measure tool to confirm the design table modification.

	$DESCRIPTION	$COLOR	X@Sketch3	Y@Sketch5	$STATE@Sketch15	$STATE@Boss-Extrude4	$STATE@Cut-Extrude3	$STATE@Fillet3	$STATE@Cut-Extrude5	$STATE@Fillet4
sample6-1	sample6-1	5659017	76.33333333	87.33333333	S	S				
sample6-2	sample6-2	15266559	76.33333333	87.33333333	S	S				
sample6-3	sample6-3	16771293	76.33333333	87.33333333	S	S				
sample6-4	sample6-4	16771293	76.33333333	87.33333333	S	S	S	S	S	S
sample6-5	sample6-5	5659017	76.33333333	87.33333333						
sample6-6	sample6-6	15266559	76.33333333	87.33333333	S	S				

Design Table for: Sample6

	$DESCRIPTION	$COLOR	X@Sketch3	Y@Sketch5	$STATE@Sketch15	$STATE@Boss-Extrude4	$STATE@Cut-Extrude3	$STATE@Fillet3	$STATE@Cut-Extrude5	$STATE@Fillet4
sample6-1	sample6-1	5659017	76.33333333	87.33333333	S	S	U	U	U	U
sample6-2	sample6-2	15266559	76.33333333	87.33333333	S	S	U	U	U	U
sample6-3	sample6-3	16771293	76.33333333	87.33333333	S	S	U	U	U	U
sample6-4	sample6-4	16771293	76.33333333	87.33333333	S	S	S	S	S	S
sample6-5	sample6-5	5659017	76.33333333	87.33333333	U	U	U	U	U	U
sample6-6	sample6-6	15266559	76.33333333	87.33333333	S	S	U	U	U	U

Design Table for: Sample6

D1@Boss-Extrude1

Dist: 35mm

Design Table for: Sample6

	$DESCRIPTION	$COLOR	X@Sketch3	@Sketch5	$STATE@Sketch15	$STATE@Boss-Extrude4	$STATE@Cut-Extrude3	$STATE@Fillet3	$STATE@Cut-Extrude5	$STATE@Fillet4	$STATE@Boss-Extrude1	D1@Boss-Extrude1
sample6-1	sample6-1	5659017	76.33333333	87.33333333	S	S	U	U	U	U	U	25
sample6-2	sample6-2	15266559	76.33333333	87.33333333	S	S	U	U	U	U	U	
sample6-3	sample6-3	16771293	76.33333333	87.33333333	S	S	U	U	U	U	U	
sample6-4	sample6-4	16771293	76.33333333	87.33333333	S	S	S	S	S	S	U	
sample6-5	sample6-5	5659017	76.33333333	87.33333333	U	U	U	U	U	U	U	
sample6-6	sample6-6	15266559	76.33333333	87.33333333	S	S	U	U	U	U	U	35

Change the following parameters in the design table for configuration sample6-6:

- A@Sketch1 = 230

- B@Sketch1 = 225

12. **Edit** the design table. Do not add any columns and rows to the table at this time. View the updated design table.

	$DESCRIPTION	$COLOR	X@Sketch3	Y@Sketch5	$STATE@Sketch15	$STATE@Boss-Extrude4	$STATE@Cut-Extrude3	$STATE@Fillet3	$STATE@Cut-Extrude5	$STATE@Fillet4	$STATE@Boss-Extrude1	D1@Boss-Extrude1
Design Table for: Sample6												
sample6-1	sample6-1	5659017	76.33333333	87.33333333	U	U	U	U	U	U	U	25
sample6-2	sample6-2	15266559	76.33333333	87.33333333	S	S	U	U	U	U	U	25
sample6-3	sample6-3	16771293	76.33333333	87.33333333	U	U	U	U	U	U	U	25
sample6-4	sample6-4	16771293	76.33333333	87.33333333	U	U	S	S	S	S	U	25
sample6-5	sample6-5	5659017	76.33333333	87.33333333	U	U	U	U	U	U	U	25
sample6-6	sample6-6	15266559	76.33333333	87.33333333	S	S	U	U	U	U	U	35

13. **Double-click** the front face of Boss-Extrude1 in the Graphics window. Dimensions A and B are displayed.

14. **Double-click** inside cell N2.

15. **Double-click** dimension A in the Graphics window. Click OK.

16. **Double-click** inside cell O2.

17. **Double-click** dimension B in the Graphics window. Click OK. View the updated design table.

18. **Double-click** inside cell N8.

19. **Enter** 230 as illustrated.

20. **Double-click** inside cell O8.

21. **Enter** 225 as illustrated.

	A	B	C	D	E	F	G	H	I	J	K	L	M	N	O
1	Design Table for: Sample6														
2		$DESCRIPTION	$COLOR	X@Sketch3	Y@Sketch5	$STATE@Sketch15	$STATE@Boss-Extrude4	$STATE@Cut-Extrude3	$STATE@Fillet3	$STATE@Cut-Extrude5	$STATE@Fillet4	$STATE@Boss-Extrude1	D1@Boss-Extrude1	A@Sketch1	B@Sketch1
3	sample6-1	sample6-1	5659017	76.33333333	87.33333333	U	U	U	U	U	U	U		25	229	217
4	sample6-2	sample6-2	15266559	76.33333333	87.33333333	S	S	U	U	U	U	U		25		
5	sample6-3	sample6-3	16771293	76.33333333	87.33333333	U	U	U	U	U	U	U		25		
6	sample6-4	sample6-4	16771293	76.33333333	87.33333333	U	U	S	S	S	S	U		25		
7	sample6-5	sample6-5	5659017	76.33333333	87.33333333	U	U	U	U	U	U	U		25		
8	sample6-6	sample6-6	15266559	76.33333333	87.33333333	S	S	U	U	U	U	U		35	230	225
9															
10															
11															
12															
13															
14															
15															
16															
17															
18															
19															
20															

22. **Exit** the design table.

23. **Double-click** sample6-6. Sample6-6 is the active configuration.

24. **Double-click** on the Boss-Extrude1 feature. View the modified dimensions.

25. **Calculate** the Mass Properties of configuration sample6-6.

26. **Enter 16604.47** grams for the anwser. In the CSWP exam you will need to enter this number exactly. You are finished with the first category in Segment 2 of the CSWP CORE exam.

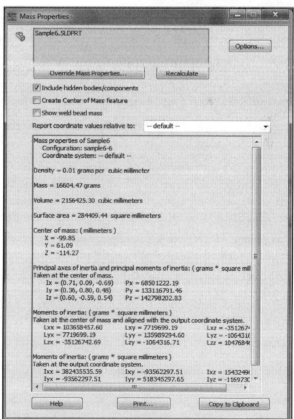

Second Category:

- Modify features and sketches of an existing part

- Recover from rebuild errors while maintaining the overall design intent

In the second category read question 7 and 8 carefully.

Click the link which will download the needed document.

Create a folder to save your working models.

Modify a part and recover from errors in this category. Edges, fillets and faces will be lost and modify planes and sketches.

Copy the CSWP Folder from the DVD to your hard drive. Open the sample7-1 part from the Segment 2 Initial folder. This will be your downloaded part for this segment.

Let's begin.

A question in this section could be - determine the mass of the part in grams.

Decimal places: 2.

The questions start off simple and then increase in difficulty. Remember Segment 2 is only 40 minutes long.

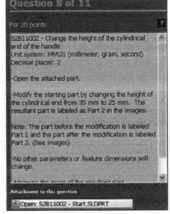

Actual CSWP exam format

1. **Open** the Sample7-1 part from the Segment 2 Initial folder.

2. **Calculate** the mass of the part in grams.

3. **Select 1443.72** grams in the multiple-choice answer section of the exam. The first question in this segment is typically in a multiple choice format.

4. **Save** Sample7-1 as Sample7-2.

A question in this section could be - modify the large hole diameter from 25mm to 20mm.

Calculate the mass of the part in grams.

Let's begin.

First find the large hole and its initial value.

5. **Double-click** Cut-Extrude1. View the 25mm diameter.

```
Mass = 1443.72 grams
Volume = 185092.66 cubic millimeters
Surface area = 40693.25 square millimeters
Center of mass: ( millimeters )
   X = 8.31
   Y = -10.49
   Z = -0.78
```

6. **Enter** 20mm.

7. **Rebuild** the part.

8. **Calculate** the mass of the part in grams.

9. **Enter 1522.29** grams. Think about your answer. If you obtain a lower mass number when you have more material, something is wrong.

10. **Save** Sample7-2 as Sample7-3.

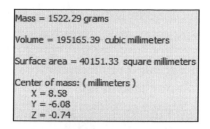

A question in this section could be - modify the shell thickness from 5mm to 4mm.

Calculate the mass of the part in grams.

Decimal places: 2.

Think about the effects of this modification on the mass of the part.

Let's begin.

11. **Edit** Shell1 from the FeatureManager.

12. **Enter** 4mm for Thickness.

13. **Calculate** the mass of the part in grams.

14. **Enter 961.25** grams.

15. **Save** Sample7-3 as Sample7-4.

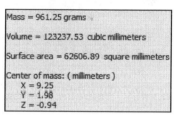

A question in this section could be - create a symmetrical handle between the two cylinders.

The handle is symmetrical both horizontally and vertically.

Delete the Shell feature.

Maintain the original fillet dimension in the handle of 20mm. Maintain the overall dimension between the two cylinders of 150mm.

Calculate the mass of the part in grams.

SolidWorks will present multiple views of the model in the question (an overall view of the sketch) or the overall depth of the feature.

View the segment videos and model folders provided in the book for additional procedure and detail information.

Let's begin. Start with your Sample7-4 model.

1. **Suppress** the Shell1 feature from the FeatureManager. As a general rule, suppress features before you delete them. This will inform you if there are any rebuild or feature errors during modification in the exam.

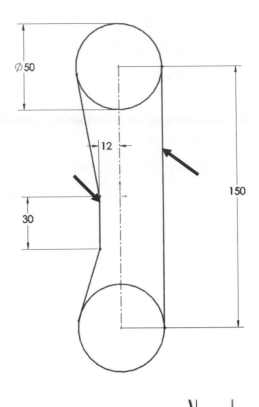

2. **Edit** Sketch1 (Multi-body sketch) from the Boss-Extrude2 feature in the FeatureManager. View the dimensions. Keep the 150mm dimension.

3. **Delete** any unneeded geometric relations (Horizontal) or sketch entities (vertical line) as illustrated. Deleting the Horizontal relation on the point provides the ability to move the attached sketch entities.

4. **Create** a horizontal centerline between the origin and the midpoint of the vertical line to the left of the origin.

5. **Insert** a Horizontal relation as illustrated. As a general rule, insert geometric relations before dimensions in a sketch.

There are numerous ways to address the models in this book. A goal is to display different design intents and techniques for a timed exam.

The question was to create a symmetrical handle between the two cylinders. The handle is symmetrical both horizontally and vertically. Add a symmetric relation.

6. **Select** the Centerline, the two end points on the sketch and add a symmetric relation.

Sketch1 is fully defined. Mirror the sketch to the right side.

7. **Window-select** the sketch on the left side and apply the Mirror Entities Sketch tool. Mirror about the vertical centerline. The sketch is fully defined.

The width between the two vertical lines in the initial question displayed a sketch that showed 28mm.

8. **Modify** the 12mm dimension to 14mm to obtain the needed width.

Address all needed fillet features. Maintain the original fillet dimension in the handle of 20mm.

9. **Edit** the Fillet1 feature. Select the two edges. Four edges should be displayed in the Fillet1 PropertyManager.

10. **Calculate** the mass of the part in grams.

11. **Enter 1576.76** grams.

12. **Save** Sample7-4 as Sample7-5.

☀ Utilize the segment videos and model folders provided to follow along while using the book. Each segment video provides valuable information to successfully pass the CSWP CORE exam.

☀ SolidWorks Mass Properties calculates the center of mass for every model. At every instant of time, there is a unique location (x, y, z) in space that is the average position of the systems mass. The CSWP exam asks for center of gravity. For the purpose of calculating the center of mass and center of gravity near to earth or on earth, you can assume that the center of mass and the center of gravity are the same.

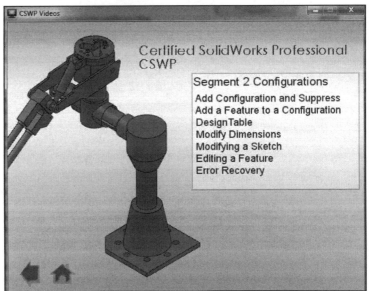

☀ This section presents a representation of the types of questions that you will see in this segment of the exam.

☀ Always save your models to verify your results.

A question in this section could be - modify the depth of the Boss-Extrude3 feature.

Modify the height from 57mm to 47mm. This would mean that the height of the smaller boss is 17mm.

Delete the Shell feature.

Calculate the mass of the part in grams.

Decimal places: 2.

This looks like a straight forward problem. Be careful. SolidWorks wants you to understand how to create features and their options.

Let's begin.

Start with the Sample7-5 model. In Sample7-5, the Shell1 feature is suppressed.

1. **Edit** Boss-Extrude3 from the FeatureManager. Note the sketch is not created from the base of the larger cylinder. The Start Condition is Offset. The End Condition is Up To Surface. The two circular sketches were created on Plane1.

2. **Enter** 2mm (you need 47mm - Offset by 12 - reduce it to 2mm) in the Enter Offset Value box to obtain the needed value.

Confirm that your math is correct. Use the Measure tool during the exam.

3. **Calculate** the mass of the part in grams.

4. **Enter 1401.30** grams. You need to be within 1% of the answer to get this question correct.

5. **Save** Sample7-5 as Sample7-6.

A question in this section could be - modify the sketch on the bottom cylinder to a 21mm square, centered on the cylindrical feature as illustrated.

The square boss contains no fillets.

Maintain all dimensions for both the 10mm and 5mm thru holes as illustrated.

Calculate the mass of the part in grams.

Decimal places: 2.

Think about the feature that you need to delete.

Will there be rebuild errors that you need to address?

Study the provided views and read the question carefully. Remember, there is no partial credit.

Let's begin.

Start with your model Sample7-6.

Delete the original Sketch entities. You need to modify the sketch on the bottom cylinder to a 21mm square, centered on the cylindrical feature.

6. **Edit** Sketch2 from the Boss-Extrude3 feature.

7. **Window-select** the bottom cylinder sketch entities as illustrated.

8. **Press** Delete.

9. **Click** Yes.

10. **Create** a Center Rectangle sketch located at the center point of the Boss-Extrude1 feature as illustrated.

11. **Insert** needed geometric relations and dimension.

You deleted a circular face to create a square face. A rebuild error is displayed. The sketch contains dimensions or relations to model geometry which no longer exists.

12. **Click** Stop and Repair.

13. **Repair** the Fillet3 feature. You deleted the sketch geometry when you created the center rectangle.

14. **Repair** the Plane2 feature. Plane2 used the small cylindrical face which was deleted. Use the large cylindrical face to repair.

15. **Repair** the Cut-Extrude1 feature. Edit Sketch3. Delete (Coincident1) a dangling sketch entity.

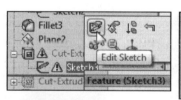

16. **Insert** a Concentric relation to fully define Sketch3. Sketch3 is fully defined. Exit the sketch.

Sketch4 contains dimensions or relations to model geometry which no longer exists. Address Sketch4.

17. **Edit** the Sketch Plane of Sketch4. The original Sketch plane was located on the cylindrical face of Boss-Extrude3 which was modified. Select a new Sketch Plane.

18. A SolidWorks dialog box is displayed. **Press** the Continue (Ignore Error) button.

There are still a few dangling relations associated with the small hole (Cut-Extrude2).

19. **Edit** Sketch4. Delete the Coincident0 and Distance2 relation.

20. **Fully define** Sketch4. Insert the needed dimension and Coincident relation. The hole should be centered on the Boss-Extrude3 feature.

You now have a clean part with no error messages.

21. **Calculate** the mass of the part in grams.

22. **Enter 1278.37** grams. You need to be within 1% of the answer to get this question correct.

You are finished with the Segment 2 section in this chapter. The questions in this Segment are not too difficult but you only have 40 minutes for this segment. Managing your time is key in any segment of the CSWP CORE exam.

At the end of the exam, view the Summary dialog box. Press the End Examination button only if you are finished.

Utilize the segment videos and model folders provided to follow along while using the book. Each segment video provides valuable information to successfully pass the CSWP CORE exam.

There are numerous ways to address the model in this section. A goal is to display different design intents and techniques.

Always save your models to verify your results.

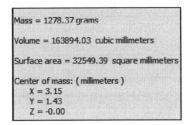

Mass = 1278.37 grams

Volume = 163894.03 cubic millimeters

Surface area = 32549.39 square millimeters

Center of mass: (millimeters)
  X = 3.15
  Y = 1.43
  Z = -0.00

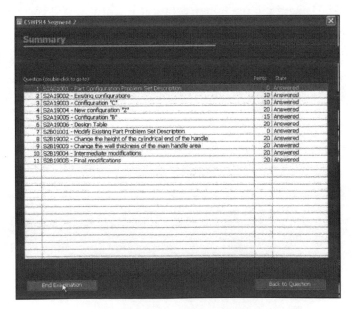

Actual CSWP
exam format

A total score of 115 out of 155 or better is required to pass the second segment. When you pass the second segment of the CSWP CORE exam you receive the following email. Click on the SolidWorks Certification Center hyperlink to login, activate and view your certificate.

Congratulations David!
You have been issued a certificate in SolidWorks® Virtual Test Center indicating that you have successfully completed the requirements for **Segment 2 of Certified SolidWorks Professional Core.**

CertificateID: ·

Visit your certificate area on SolidWorks® Certification Center. Click My Account to access your certificates and exams.

Congratulations,
Avelino Rochino

SolidWorks® is a registered trademark of Dassault Systèmes SolidWorks Corp.

For many features in SolidWorks 2013 and newer (Extruded Boss/Base, Extruded Cut, Simple Hole, Revolved Boss/Base, Revolved Cut, Fillet, Chamfer, Scale, Shell, Rib, Circular Pattern, Linear Pattern, Curve Driven Pattern, Revolved Surface, Extruded Surface, Fillet Surface, Edge Flange and Base Flange) you can enter and modify equations directly in the PropertyManager fields that allow numerical inputs.

You can create equations with global variables, functions, and file properties without accessing the Equations, Global Variables and Dimensions dialog box.

For example, in the PropertyManager for the Extruded Boss/Base feature, you can enter equations in:

- Depth fields for Direction 1 and Direction 2

- Draft fields for Direction 1 and Direction 2

- Thickness fields for a Thin Feature with two direction types

- Offset Distance field

To create an equation in a numeric input field, start by entering = (equal sign). A drop-down list displays options for global variables, functions, and file properties. Numeric input fields that contain equations can display either the equation itself or its evaluated value.

You can toggle between the equation and the value by clicking the Equations or Global Variable button that appears at the beginning of the field.

In SolidWorks 2013 or newer, right-click anywhere on an extruded feature and change the end condition from the shortcut menu. Click in empty space, on geometry, or on the handle. The shortcut menu provides all the options for Direction 1 and Direction 2. Note: Options are document dependent.

The Modify dimension box can accept equations (SW 2013 and newer). You can also use it to create on-the fly global variables. To start an equation in the Modify box, start by replacing the numeric value with an = in the value box. When you do this, you will see a

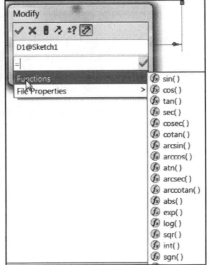

drop-down from functions and file properties. You can also us the dimension entry boxes in the PropertyManager.

Segment 2 - First category of the CSWP CORE exam - Additional Practice Problems

In this section, there are fewer step-by-step procedures. Utilize the rollback bar if needed in the provided initial and final models.

Question 1:
A question in this section could be - How many configurations are there associated with this part?

Let's begin.

1. **Open** the CSWP PP 4-1 part from the Segment 2 Initial folder.

2. **Click** the ConfigurationManager tab in the design tree. View the different configurations of the part.

3. **Select** 3 for the number of configurations in the multiple-choice answer section of the exam. The first question in this segment is typically in a multiple choice format.

a) 1, b) 2, c) **3,** d) 4

4. **Save** the model.

☀ Double-click on each configuration in the ConfigurationManager. The FeatureManager displays a different material for each configuration. It is important that you understand that these materials will change in the exam and to understand where you would start a new configuration to the existing ConfigurationManager.

Question 1: Part II
A question in this section could be - calculate the mass in grams of configuration Example 4-2.

Provided Information:

Decimal places: 2.

Let's begin.

1. **Double-click** Example 4-2. Example 4-2 is the active configuration.

2. **Calculate** the mass of the Example 4-2 configuration in grams.

3. **Enter 1229.65** grams for the answer. It is very important to input the proper decimal places as requested in the exam. In this case (2) two.

4. **Save** the model.

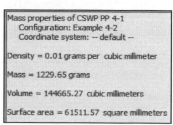

Mass properties of CSWP PP 4-1
Configuration: Example 4-2
Coordinate system: -- default --

Density = 0.01 grams per cubic millimeter

Mass = 1229.65 grams

Volume = 144665.27 cubic millimeters

Surface area = 61511.57 square millimeters

Question 3:

A question in this section could be - create a new configuration named Example 4-4 based on the Example 4-3 configuration.

Modify the design table with the specified values.

- D1@Sketch1=70
- D2@Sketch1=50
- D3@Sketch1=46
- D5@Extrude-Thin1=30
- D1@Shell1=8
- D1@Sketch2=12
- Cut-Extrude3=Suppressed
- Cut-Extrude4=Unsuppressed

Calculate the mass of the part (Example 4-4 configuration) in grams.

Decimal places: 2.

Let's begin.

1. **If needed, click** the ConfigurationManager tab in the design tree to view the different configurations of the part.

2. **Double-click** the Example 4-3 configuration. This is the active configuration.

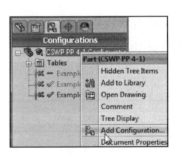

3. **Add** a new Configuration named Example 4-4.

4. **Edit** the Design Table. Modify the design table with the new specified values.

	$DESCRIPTION	$PARTNUMBER	$COLOR	D1@Sketch1	D2@Sketch1	D3@Sketch1	D4@Sketch1	D1@Extrude-Thin1	D5@Extrude-Thin1	D1@Shell1	D1@Sketch2	D1@Sketch3	$STATE@Boss-Extrude2	$STATE@Sketch3	$STATE@Cut-Extrude1	$STATE@Mirror1	$STATE@Boss-Extrude3	$STATE@Cut-Extrude2	$STATE@Mirror2	$STATE@Mirror3	$STATE@Cut-Extrude3	$STATE@Cut-Extrude4	$STATE@Sketch5
Example 4-1	Example 4-1	$C	14873855	60	60	25	45	65	20	10	10	10	U	U	U	U	S	S	S	S	U	S	S
Example 4-2	Example 4-2	$C	33957	50	60	35	45	75	20	5	8	5	U	U	U	U	S	S	S	S	U	S	S
Example 4-3	Example 4-3	$C	9211015	50	60	35	45	75	20	5	8	5	S	S	S	S	U	U	U	U	U	S	U
Example 4-4	Example 4-4	$D	9211015	50	60	35	45	75	20	5	8	5	S	S	S	S	U	U	U	U	U	S	U

Design Table for: CSWP PP 4-1

Sheet1

	$DESCRIPTION	$PARTNUMBER	$COLOR	D1@Sketch1	D2@Sketch1	D3@Sketch1	D4@Sketch1	D1@Extrude-Thin1	D5@Extrude-Thin1	D1@Shell1	D1@Sketch2	D1@Sketch3	$STATE@Boss-Extrude2	$STATE@Sketch3	$STATE@Cut-Extrude1	$STATE@Mirror1	$STATE@Boss-Extrude3	$STATE@Cut-Extrude2	$STATE@Mirror2	$STATE@Mirror3	$STATE@Cut-Extrude3	$STATE@Cut-Extrude4	$STATE@Sketch5
Design Table for: CSWP PP 4-1																							
Example 4-1	Example 4-1	$C	14873855	60	60	25	45	65	20	10	10	10	U	U	U	U	S	S	S	S	U	S	S
Example 4-2	Example 4-2	$C	33957	50	60	35	45	75	20	5	8	5	U	U	U	U	S	S	S	S	U	S	S
Example 4-3	Example 4-3	$C	9211015	50	60	35	45	75	20	5	8	5	S	S	S	S	U	U	U	U	S	U	
Example 4-4	Example 4-4	$C	9211015	70	50	46	45	75	30	8	12	5	S	S	S	S	U	U	U	U	S	U	U

Sheet1

5. **Exit** the Design Table.

6. **Calculate** the mass of the part (Example 4-4 configuration) in grams.

7. **Enter 2663.48** grams for the answer. You need to be within 1% of the stated value in the single answer format to get this question correct. It is also very important to input the proper decimal places as requested in the exam. In this case there are (2) two. Round your answers if needed.

8. **Save** the part.

Mass properties of CSWP PP 4-1 Final
Configuration: Example 4-4
Coordinate system: -- default --

Density = 0.01 grams per cubic millimeter

Mass = 2663.48 grams

Volume = 341471.93 cubic millimeters

Surface area = 93551.54 square millimeters

Center of mass: (millimeters)
  X = 141.00
  Y = -4.95
  Z = 0.00

CSWP PP 4-1 Final (Example 4-4<Display
- Sensors
- Annotations
- Plain Carbon Steel
- Front Plane
- Top Plane
- Right Plane
- Origin
- Extrude-Thin1
- Cut-Extrude4
- Shell1
- Boss-Extrude2
- Cut-Extrude1
- Plane1
- Mirror1
- Fillet1
- Fillet2
- Boss-Extrude3
- Cut-Extrude2
- Mirror2
- Mirror3
- Cut-Extrude3

Segment 2 - Second category of the CSWP CORE exam - Additional Practice Problems

In this section, there are fewer step-by-step procedures. Utilize the rollback bar if needed in the provided initial and final models.

Question 1:

A question in this section could be - modify part CSWP PP5-1 per the provided drawing information.

What is the mass of the new part?

All holes through all unless shown otherwise.

Units: MMGS (millimeters, grams, second)

Decimal Places: 2

Part Origin: Arbitrary

Material: Cast Alloy Steel

Density: 7300 kg/m^2

Part CSWP PP5-1 Initial

Part CSWP PP5-1 Final

Let's begin.

1. **Create** a folder to save your working model.

2. **Open** the CSWP PP5-1 part from the Segment 2 Initial folder.

3. **View** the FeatureManager. Use the Rollbar bar to examine and modify features and sketches from the provided drawing information.

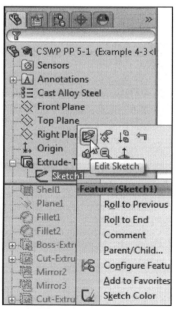

4. **Modify** the Extrude-Thin1 sketch as illustrated using a 3point Arc Sketch tool. Both sketches are fully defined. Dimensions and geometric relations define the sketches. The drawing views provide the needed information for sketch and feature modification of the part.

5. **Exit** the sketch. Continue and ignore any errors.

6. **Move** the rollback bar down below the Shell1 feature. Shell1 displays an error in the FeatureManager.

7. **Edit** the Shell feature (Shell1).
   Remove the missing faces and select
   the face of the arc to address the error.

8. **Move** the rollback bar down below
   the Fillet2 feature. Fillet2 displays
   an error in the FeatureManager.

9. **Edit** the second Fillet feature
   (Fillet2). Remove the missing edges
   and update the edges where the arc
   and the lines meet as illustrated.

10. **Move** the rollback bar down below the Cut-Extrude4 feature in the FeatureManager. The sketch for Cut-Extrude4 contains dimensions or relations to model geometry which no longer exist.

11. **Edit** the Sketch plane for the Cut-Extrude4 feature. There are missing items in the feature. Remove the missing plane.

12. **Select** Top Plane for the sketch plane. Remember the provided drawing information. An Extruded-Cut feature is needed on the top of the arc.

13. **Continue** and ignore any errors. Close the What's Wrong dialog box.

14. **Center** the hole on the part as illustrated. Delete the midpoint relation and add a dimension of 115mm from the center of the hole to the side edge of the part.

15. **Move** the Cut-Extrude4 feature before the Shell1 feature in the FeatureManager as illustrated.

16. **View** the results in the Graphics window.

17. **Edit** the Boss-Extrude3 sketch (Sketch4). Modify the sketch per the provided information in the drawing.

18. **Continue** and ignore any errors. Close the What's Wrong dialog box.

19. **Edit** Sketch5. Modify the location of the center hole. Delete the Coincident relation with the center of the circle. Drag the center of the circle so that it is Coincident with the center of the corner fillet.

20. **Modify** the diameter of the hole from 6mm to 8mm. Exit the Sketch.

21. **Calculate** the mass of the part in grams.

22. **Enter** 1088.85 grams.

23. **Save** the part.

You are finished with this section. Good luck on the exam in Segment 2.

There are numerous ways to build the model in this section. A goal is to display different design intents and techniques.

Below are former screen shots from a previous CSWP exam in Segment 2.

CHAPTER 3 - SEGMENT 3 OF THE CSWP CORE EXAM

Introduction

The third segment is 80 minutes with twelve (12) questions (13 total but one is an instructional page). The format is either multiple choice or single fill in the blank. The first question in this segment is typically in a multiple choice format.

This section presents a representation of the types of questions that you will see in this segment of the exam.

Utilize the segment videos and model folders to follow along while using the book. Each segment video provides valuable information to successfully pass the CSWP CORE exam.

Questions 2 through 13 ask you to perform the following general tasks:

- Create a simple component and sub-assembly

- Download parts and assemble components and a sub-assembly into an assembly

- Insert Width, Angle, Parallel, Distance, and other mate types

- Calculate interference detection and measure distances and angles

- Modify mates

- Replace components in the assembly

Actual CSWP
exam format

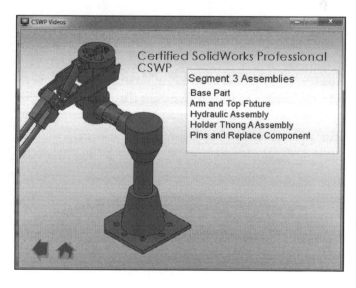

- Determine center of gravity based on a unique reference coordinate system and total mass of the assembly

For these tasks, review the text and the five (5) videos on the DVD that correspond to the competencies you need to know for segment 3 of the CSWP CORE exam.

A total score of 140 out of 190 or better is required to pass the third segment. When you pass the third segment of the CSWP CORE exam you will receive the following email.

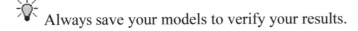

Congratulations David!
You have been issued a certificate in SolidWorks® Virtual Test Center indicating that you have successfully completed the requirements for **Segment 3 of Certified SolidWorks Professional Core.**

CertificateID: C-

Visit your certificate area on SolidWorks® Certification Center. Click My Account to access your certificates and exams.

Congratulations,
Avelino Rochino

Click on the SolidWorks Certification Center hyperlink to login, activate and view your certificate.

Utilize the DVD (segment videos and model folders) to follow along while using the book. Each segment video provides valuable information to successfully pass the CSWP CORE exam.

☀ Screen shots in the book were made using SolidWorks 2012, 2013 and 2014 SP2 running Windows® 7.

☀ Always save your models to verify your results.

☀ There are numerous ways to address the question in this section. A goal is to display different design intents and techniques.

Segment 3 of the CSWP Core Exam

Create an assembly (Welding Arm) starting with the Base1 component. Some components in the exam are modeled by you and others will be supplied to you.

Load the Testing client and read the instructions. Create a folder to save your working models.

The first question in this segment is instructional as illustrated.

The second question can be - build the Base1 component for the assembly.

Calculate the mass of the Base1 part in grams.

Information on the Base1 part is provided to you in a variety of drawing views, (similar to the Segment 1 CSWP CORE) exam.

Provided information:

Unit system: MMGS (millimeter, gram, second)

Decimal place: 2

Material of Base1: Cast Stainless Steel

Density: 0.0077 g/m^3

Part origin: Arbitrary

All holes through all unless shown otherwise.

Note: Base1 is displayed in an Isometric view.

View 1:

Actual CSWP
exam format

Base1

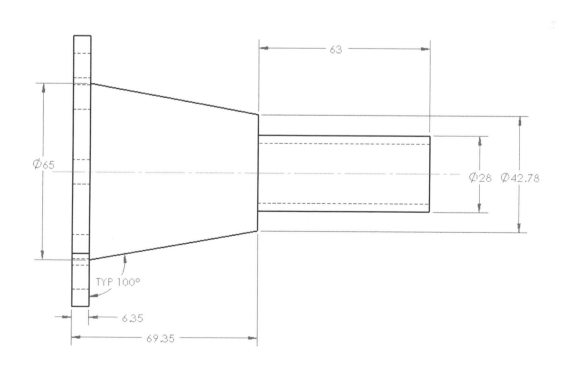

View 2:

Details are very important. Note the location of the top seed feature (Cut-Extrude1) located along the Y-axis in the drawing view. The Chamfer feature is located in the lower corner. This is important when you insert the Base1 component into the assembly document to calculate the center of gravity relative to the specified coordinate system location.

Chamfer feature

Take your time to first identify the drawing views and to better understand the provided geometry that is needed to create the initial part.

There are numerous ways to build this model.

The images displayed on the exam are not to scale due to differences in the parts being downloaded for each tester.

SolidWorks will provide a part to create that is not orientated correctly in the assembly. Knowledge of component orientation in an assembly is required along with creating a new coordinate system.

Let's begin.

Create the Base1 part. View the provided model and drawing information for dimensions and material type. Set document units and precision. The first component in an assembly should be fixed to the origin or fully defined.

1. **Create** a folder to save your working models.

2. **Set** document properties (drafting standard, units and precision) for the model.

3. **Create** Sketch1 for Base1 on the Right Plane per the illustrated Isometric view.

4. **Create** the Extruded Base (6.35 Depth) feature.

5. **Apply** material type, Cast Stainless Steel.

6. **Create** the Revolve1 feature using Sketch2 on the Front Plane (69.35mm - 6.35mm).

7. **Create** the first Extruded Cut feature (seed) for the circular pattern.

8. **Create** the Circular pattern (8 Instances) feature.

9. **Create** the Boss-Extrude feature (63mm Depth) with the needed sketch relations and dimensions.

10. **Create** the Chamfer feature.

11. **Calculate** the mass in grams.

12. **Select 1690.78** grams in the multiple-choice answer section of the exam. The first question in this segment is typically in a multiple choice format.

13. **Save** the part. Name it Base1.

It is good practice to save frequently and to rename the part or assembly if you need to go back during the exam.

You should have the exact answer (within 1% of the stated value in the multiple choice section) before you move on to the next question. If you don't have the exact answer of the first question, you will most likely fail the following question. This is crucial as there is no partial credit.

A question in this segment could be - create an Assembly document from the Base1 component.

Calculate the center of gravity in mm of the assembly relative to the new coordinate system (Coordinate System1).

Provided Information:

Unit system: MMGS (millimeter, gram, second)

Decimal places: 2

Assembly origin: Arbitrary

Orientate the Base1 component as illustrated. Create a coordinate system in the lower left corner vertex of the Base1 component as illustrated. Use this coordinate system throughout the problem sct.

SolidWorks will provide a part to create that is not orientated correctly in the assembly. Knowledge of component orientation in an assembly is required along with creating coordinate systems.

Let's begin.

1. **Create** an assembly document and insert the Base1 part. By default the Base1 component is fixed to the origin.

There are numerous ways to modify the orientation of a component in an assembly document that is fixed to the origin.

Use the Float and Mate tools in the next section. Re-orientate the Base1 component as needed. Fully define the component in the Assembly document.

2. **Float** the part. The part is free to translate or rotate in the Assembly document (six degrees of freedom).

3. **Re-orientate** the assembly as needed. Create a mate between the Top Plane of the Assembly and the top face of the Base1 component.

4. **Click** the Aligned option.

The Chamfer feature is located in the wrong corner.

5. **Create** a mate between the Front Plane of the Assembly and the Top Plane of the Base1 component. The Base1 component is able to translate along the X axis.

Another mate is needed to fully define the component.

6. **Create** a mate between the Right Plane of the Assembly and the Front Plane of the Base1 component. The Base1 component is fully defined in the Assembly document with three Coincident mates.

☀ You can also rotate the Base1 component in the assembly using the Rotate Component tool (about Y & X). View the provided media files for additional information.

Create the coordinate system to calculate the center of mass for the assembly.

7. **Click** the Coordinate System tool from the Reference Geometry drop-down menu. The Coordinate System PropertyManager is displayed.

8. **Click** the lower front right vertex for the origin.

9. **Click** the bottom front edge for the X axis.

10. **Click** the bottom right edge for the Y axis. View the new coordinate system.

11. **Calculate** the center of gravity relative to the new coordinate system (Coordinate System1).

12. **Enter** the center of gravity (mm) in the three blank fields. You need to be within 1% of the answer to get this question correct.

   X = -49.75

   Y = 50.25

   Z = 29.96

13. **Save** the assembly. In this example name the assembly Welding Arm.

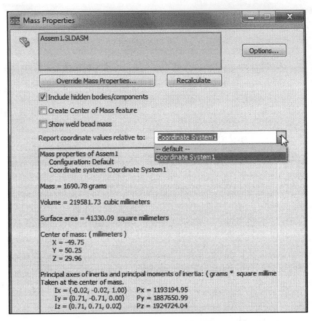

SolidWorks Mass Properties calculates the center of mass for every model. At every instant of time, there is a unique location (x, y, z) in space that is the average position of the systems mass. The CSWP exam asks for center of gravity. For the purpose of calculating the center of mass and center of gravity near to earth or on earth, you can assume that the center of mass and the center of gravity are the same.

There are numerous ways to build the model in this section. A goal is to display different design intents and techniques.

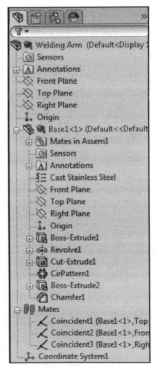

A question in this segment could be - download and open the attached assemblies.

Insert them into the Welding Arm assembly. Position the assemblies (Arm and TopFixture-A) with respect to the Base1 component as illustrated.

Create all required mates.

Calculate the center of gravity in mm of the Welding Arm assembly utilizing the created coordinate system (Coordinate System1).

💡 Imported components have imported geometry. Select "No" on Feature Recognition. Import the geometry as quickly as possible.

Provided Information:

Unit system: MMGS (millimeter, gram, second)

Decimal places: 2

SolidWorks provides symbols to indicate a Parallel mate, Width mate, Coincident mate, etc. in the exam. Take your time to review the drawing views and to understand the required mates between each component.

In this example a Parallel mate is needed between the Front Plane of the Arm sub-assembly and the front narrow face of the Base1 component.

Select your mate and you are finished. This new mate behavior is similar to the way you add sketch relations, in that it only presents mates that are valid for the items selected.

TopFixture-A Assembly

A Parallel mate is also needed between the right flat face of the TopFixture-A assembly and the right narrow face of the Base1 component.

Let's begin.

Insert the Arm assembly. Insert two Concentric mates to have the Arm free to rotate about the Base1 component.

1. **Insert** the Arm assembly (from the Segment 3 Initial/Initial 2 folder) into the Welding Arm assembly.

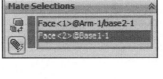

2. **Insert** a Concentric mate between the outside cylindrical face of the Arm/base2-1 and the inside cylindrical face of Base1.

3. **Insert** a Coincident mate between the bottom inside flat face of Base1 and the bottom face of Arm.

Boss-Extrude3 of base2<1>

Quick mate is a new procedure in SW 2014 to mate components together in SolidWorks. No command (click Mate from the Assembly CommandManager) needs to be executed. Just make two selections (hold the Ctrl key down between selections) and a Quick Mate pop-up appears below the context toolbar as illustrated. At this time, the quick mate procedure doesn't support complex geometry.

The Arm is free to rotate about the Base1 component. Next orientate the Arm parallel with the front narrow face of the Base1 component. Planes will be used in this section.

4. **Insert** a Parallel mate between the Front Plane of the Arm and the front narrow face of Base1.

5. **Click** the Anti-Aligned option for proper position.

Next insert the TopFixture-A assembly into the Welding Arm assembly.

6. **Insert** the TopFixture-A assembly (from the Segment 3 Initial/Initial 2 folder) into the Welding Arm assembly.

7. **Insert** a Coincident mate between the bottom face of TopFixture-A and the top face of Arm as illustrated.

8. **Insert** a Concentric mate between the cylindrical face of the Arm and the cylindrical face of TopFixture-A as illustrated. TopFixture-A is free to rotate in the Welding Arm assembly.

Boss-Extrude2 of Base4<1>

Cut-Extrude1 of midpiece<1>

Mate Selections
Face<3>@Arm-1/Base4-1
Face<4>@TopFixture-A-1/mid

9. **Insert** a Parallel mate between the right flat face of the TopFixture-A and the right narrow face of Base1.

Mate Selections
Face<5>@TopFixture-A-1/Sup
Face<6>@Base1-1

10. **Calculate** the center of gravity (mm) relative to the new coordinate system.

Parallel

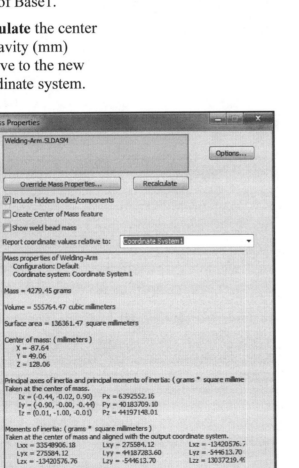

Mass Properties

Welding-Arm.SLDASM

Options...

Override Mass Properties...   Recalculate

☑ Include hidden bodies/components
☐ Create Center of Mass feature
☐ Show weld bead mass

Report coordinate values relative to: Coordinate System1

Mass properties of Welding-Arm
    Configuration: Default
    Coordinate system: Coordinate System1

Mass = 4279.45 grams

Volume = 555764.47 cubic millimeters

Surface area = 136361.47 square millimeters

Center of mass: (millimeters)
    X = -87.64
    Y = 49.06
    Z = 128.06

Principal axes of inertia and principal moments of inertia: (grams * square millime
Taken at the center of mass.
    Ix = (-0.44, -0.02, 0.90)   Px = 6392552.16
    Iy = (-0.90, -0.00, -0.44)   Py = 40183709.10
    Iz = (0.01, -1.00, -0.01)   Pz = 44197148.01

Moments of inertia: (grams * square millimeters)
Taken at the center of mass and aligned with the output coordinate system.
    Lxx = 33548906.18   Lxy = 275584.12   Lxz = -13420576.7
    Lyx = 275584.12   Lyy = 44187283.60   Lyz = -544613.70
    Lzx = -13420576.76   Lzy = -544613.70   Lzz = 13037219.49

Moments of inertia: (grams * square millimeters)
Taken at the output coordinate system.
    Ixx = 114030464.06   Ixy = -18123704.46   Ixz = -61450810.2
    Iyx = -18123704.46   Iyy = 147239804.47   Iyz = 26340671.98
    Izx = -61450810.23   Izy = 26340671.98   Izz = 56206463.77

Help   Print...   Copy to Clipboard

11. **Enter** the center of gravity (mm) in the three blank fields. You need to be within 1% of the answer to get this question correct.

X = -87.64

Y = 49.06

Z = 128.06

12. **Save** the assembly.

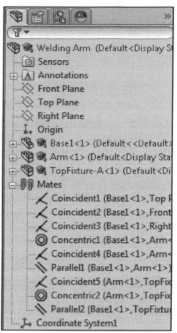

At the time of this writing, there were slight variations in Mass Properties between SolidWorks 32 bit versus 64 bit. These variations are still within the 1% required for the CSWP exam segments. Always save your models to verify your results.

SolidWorks Mass Properties calculates the center of mass for every model. At every instant of time, there is a unique location (x, y, z) in space that is the average position of the systems mass. The CSWP exam asks for center of gravity. For the purpose of calculating the center of mass and center of gravity near to earth or on earth, you can assume that the center of mass and the center of gravity are the same.

A question in this segment could be - insert the Holder-Thongs-A assembly in the Welding Arm assembly.

Insert all needed mates.

What is the distance between the right flat face of Holder-Thongs-A and the right flat face of the TopFixture-A Support in the Welding Arm assembly in mm?

Another question in this segment could be - with Collision Detection turned ON, rotate Holder-Thong-A as shown in the image until Thong is stopped by the Arm.

Calculate the angle between the flat face of Boss-Extrude1 of the Fixture and the flat face of Boss-Extrude1 of the Holder as illustrated.

Provided Information:

Unit system: MMGS (millimeter, gram, second)

Decimal places: 2

Note: Modify or delete any previously placed mates if necessary.

 Knowledge of Collision Detection and the Measure tool is required for this section.

Distance ?

Holder-Thong-A assembly Collision Detection ON

Utilize the segment videos and model folders to follow along while using the book. Each segment video provides valuable information to successfully pass the CSWP CORE exam.

Let's begin.

Insert the Holder-Thongs-A assembly. Insert a Concentric mate and a Width mate between the Holder-Thongs-A assembly and the TopFixture assembly.

1. **Insert** the Holder-Thongs-A assembly (from the Segment 3 Initial/Initial 3 folder) into the Welding Arm assembly.

2. **Insert** a Concentric mate between the inside cylindrical face of Holder-Thongs-A and the inside cylindrical face of the TopFixture.

3. **Insert** the needed Width mate between Holder-Thongs-A and TopFixture. The Holder is free to rotate.

4. **Calculate** the distance between the right flat face of Holder-Thongs-A and the right flat face of TopFixture-A Support in mm.

5. **Enter 15.48mm** for distance. You need to be within 1% of the answer to get this question correct.

6. **Save** the assembly.

You may also be required to measure angles between flat surfaces. Be certain to understand the direction, complement or supplement of the required angle.

To address the second part of the question - with Collision Detection turned ON, rotate Holder-Thong-A as illustrated until Thong is stopped by Arm.

Calculate the angle between the flat face of Boss-Extrude1 of the Fixture and flat face of Boss-Extrude1 of the Holder.

7. **Activate** Collision detection from the Rotate Component PropertyManager.

8. **Rotate** Holder-Thong-A until Thong is stopped by the Arm assembly.

9. **Calculate** the angle between the flat face of Boss-Extrude1 of the Fixture and flat face of Boss-Extrude1 of the Holder.

10. **Enter 144.84**. It is very important to input the proper decimal places as requested in the exam. In this case two (2).

Holder-Thong-A assembly

11. **Save** the assembly. Note at this time the mass of the assembly is 4557.90 grams.

If you don't find your answer (within 1%) in the multiple choice single answer format section, recheck your solid model for precision and accuracy.

A question in this segment could be - position the Holder-Thongs-A assembly so that it interferes with the TopFixture-A assembly.

Perform an Interference Detection check on the Welding Arm assembly while turning ON the following options:

Treat sub-assemblies as components. Make interfering parts transparent.

Note: All other Interference Detection Options will be unchecked (OFF).

Select ALL the components that are found to cause interferences or "No interferences detected" if no interferences are found.

12. **Activate** the Interference Detection tool. View the PropertyManager. Clear all selections. Select the entire Welding Arm assembly.

13. **Rotate** the Holder so that it interferes with the TopFixture.

14. **Calculate** the results.

Depending on the angle of rotation of the Holder-Thongs-Assembly the components that interfere are: base2, thong, Arm, and Holder-Thongs-A. In an assembly, the location of the components that are not fully constrained will determine the volume of interference.

A question in this segment could be - download and open the attached components.

Create the Hydraulic and Brace Assembly.

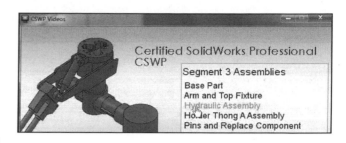

The Hydraulic and Brace Assembly consist of two components: Hydraulic1 & BRACE.

Insert a 20mm Distance mate between the bottom cylindrical face of BRACE and the bottom cylindrical face of Hydraulic1.

Calculate the mass of the assembly in grams. Save the assembly.

Later insert the assembly into the Welder Arm assembly.

Provided Information:

Unit system: MMGS (millimeter, gram, second)

Decimal places: 2

Material of components: Cast Stainless Steel

Density – 0.0077 g/m^3

Part origin: Arbitrary

Utilize the segment videos and model folders to follow along while using the book. Each segment video provides valuable information to successfully pass the CSWP CORE exam.

Let's begin.

1. **Create** the Hydraulic and Brace Assembly document.

2. **Set** document properties (drafting standard, units and precision).

3. **Insert** the Hydraulic1 component (Segment 3 Initial/Initial 4 folder). The Hydraulic1 component is fixed to the origin.

4. **Insert** the BRACE component.

5. **Create** a Concentric mate between the inside cylindrical face of Hydraulic1 and the outside cylindrical face of BRACE.

6. **Create** a Parallel mate between the outside cylindrical face of Hydraulic1 and the outside cylindrical face of BRACE.

7. **Create** a Distance mate (20mm) between the inside bottom face of Hydraulic1 and the bottom flat face of BRACE as illustrated.

8. **Calculate** the mass of the assembly in grams.

9. **Enter 51.55** grams. Always enter the needed decimal places (in this case 2) in the answer field.

10. **Save** the assembly.

Quick mate is a new procedure in SW 2014 to mate components together in SolidWorks. No command (click Mate from the Assembly CommandManager) needs to be executed. Just make two selections (hold the Ctrl key down between selections) and a Quick Mate pop-up appears below the context toolbar. At this time, the quick mate procedure doesn't support complex geometry.

A question in this segment could be - Insert the Hydraulic and Brace assembly into the Welding Arm assembly.

Suppress the Distance mate in the Hydraulic and Brace assembly.

Make the Hydraulic and Brace assembly flexible.

Mate and position the Hydraulic and Brace assembly in the Welding Arm assembly.

Set the proper faces (mates) as indicated in the images.

Insert a Width mate to properly position the Hydraulic and Brace assembly in between the mounting holes.

Insert an Angle mate of 25 degrees between the Holder-Thongs-A assembly and the TopFixture-A assembly.

Calculate the mass in grams of the Welding Arm assembly.

Another question could be - calculate the center of gravity (mm) relative to Coordinate System1.

Provided Information:

Unit system: MMGS (millimeter, gram, second)

Decimal places: 2

Hydraulic and Brace assembly

Hydraulic and
Brace assembly

Let's begin.

1. **Insert** the Hydraulic and Brace assembly into the Welding Arm assembly.

2. **Suppress** the Distance mate in the Hydraulic and Brace assembly.

3. **Create** a Concentric mate between the inside cylindrical face of the Hydraulic and Brace assembly and the inside cylindrical face of the Fixture tabs.

4. **Create** a Width mate between the two tabs (outside faces) of the Fixture and the two outside cylindrical faces of Hydraulic1. The Hydraulic and Brace assembly is free to rotate. When a sub-assembly is inserted into an assembly it is in the rigid state.

5. **Create** a Flexible state for the Hydraulic and Brace sub-assembly. Note the icon change in the Assembly FeatureManager.

The Hydraulic and Brace assembly is free to translate. Use this ability to translate and to align the end holes of the sub-assembly to the brace of the Welding Arm assembly.

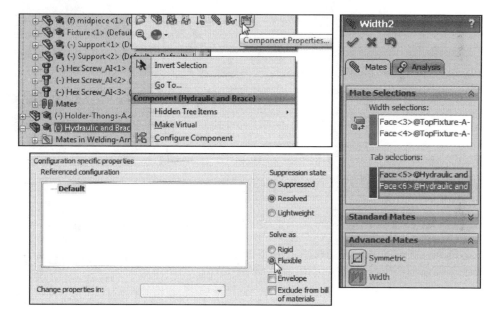

6. **Insert** a Concentric mate between the two cylindrical faces as illustrated.

7. **Insert** a (25 degree) Angle mate between the flat face of the Thong holder and the top face of the Fixture. Note: the angle dimension is referenced from the top of the Fixture.

8. **Calculate** the mass of the assembly in grams.

9. **Enter 4609.45** grams. Always enter the needed decimal places in the answer field.

10. **Calculate** the center of gravity (mm) relative to the Coordinate System1.

11. **Enter** the center of gravity (mm) in the three blank fields. You need to be within 1% of the answer to get this question correct.

    X = -92.11

    Y = 40.93

    Z = 134.49

12. **Save** the assembly.

🔆 Use the Measure tool to confirm your Angle mate dimension.

🔆 During the exam, you will be forced into an error situation. View the provided media files for additional information.

A question in this segment could be - download and open the attached components (Spring Pin Slotted _AI_1-5, Dowel Pin_AI, and Spring Pin Slotted_AI_5).

Insert the Spring Pin Slotted _AI_1-5 component, the Dowel Pin_AI component, and the Spring Pin Slotted_AI_5 component into the Welding Arm assembly.

Set the proper faces (mates) as indicated in the images.

Insert Concentric and Width mates.

Modify the dimension of the Spring Pin Slotted _AI_1-5 component to be flush with the outside face of the Support Arms (50mm).

Provided Information:

Unit system: MMGS (millimeter, gram, second)

Decimal places: 2

Calculate is the mass of the Welding Arm assembly in grams.

Spring Pin Slotted _AI_1-5

Spring Pin
Slotted_AI_5

Dowel
Pin_AI

Spring Pin
Slotted
_AI_1-5

Flush

Base-Revolve of Spring Pin Slotted_AI_5<1>

Flush

Base-Revolve of Dowel Pin_AI<1>

Flush

Let's begin.

1. **Insert** the Spring Pin Slotted _AI_1-5 component, the Dowel Pin_AI component, and the Spring Pin Slotted_AI_5 component (from Segment 3 Initial/Initial 5 - add pins folder) into the Welder Arm assembly.

2. **Create** a Concentric mate between the outside cylindrical face of the Spring Pin Slotted _AI_1-5 component and inside cylindrical face of the TopFixture-A component.

3. **Create** a Width mate between the Spring Pin Slotted _AI_1-5 component and the two support arms of the assembly. Note: the Spring Pin is not flush with the two support arms.

4. **Modify** the Spring Pin Slotted _AI_1-5 component length dimension to 50mm (flush) with the outside face of the two support arms of the assembly. It is important that you know how to modify dimensions of a component inside an assembly for the exam.

☀ Use the Measure tool to confirm your needed dimension.

Flush

5. **Create** a Concentric mate between the outside cylindrical face of the Spring Pin Slotted_AI_5 component and the inside cylindrical face of the Holder-Thongs-A component.

6. **Create** a Width mate between the Spring Pin Slotted_AI_5 component and the two faces of the Holder-Thong of the assembly. The faces are flush.

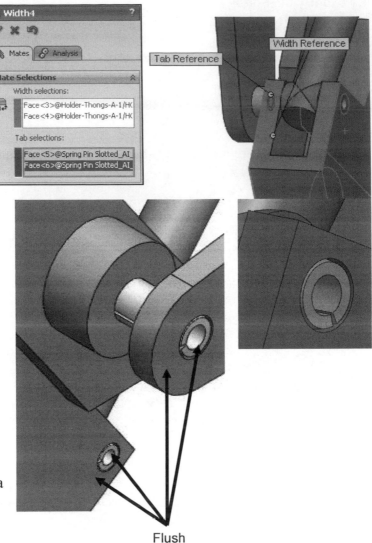

💡 Utilize the segment videos and model folders to follow along while using the book. Each segment video provides valuable information to successfully pass the CSWP CORE exam.

💡 Quick mate is a new procedure in SW 2014 to mate components together in SolidWorks. No command (click Mate from the Assembly CommandManager) needs to be executed. Just make two selections (hold the Ctrl key down between selections) and a Quick Mate pop-up appears below the context toolbar. At this time, the quick mate procedure doesn't work on complex geometry.

💡 In SW 2014, a Slot mate was added to the Mechanical Mates dialog box.

Flush

7. **Create** a Concentric mate between the outside cylindrical face of the Dowel Pin_AI component and the inside cylindrical face of the TopFixture-A component.

8. **Create** a Width mate between the Dowel Pin_AI component and the two faces. The faces are flush.

9. **Calculate** the mass of the assembly in grams.

10. **Enter 4623.00** grams. Always enter the needed decimal places in the answer field.

Another question could be - calculate the center of gravity (mm) of the Welding Arm assembly relative to Coordinate System1.

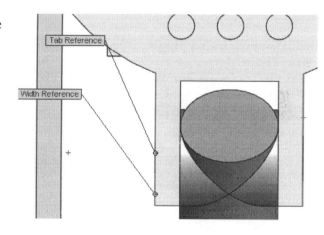

11. **Calculate** the center of gravity (mm) relative to the Coordinate System1. Enter the center of mass in the three blank fields in the exam.

   X = -92.28

   Y – 40.82

   Z = 134.84

12. **Save** the assembly.

Flush ──►

A question in this segment could be - download and open the attached component (BaseB).

Replace the Base1 component with the BaseB component.

Mate the Arm to BaseB using the same mates as with the Base1 component.

Maintain the same mates of the rest of the components as previously directed.

Redefine Coordinate System1 with BaseB as illustrated.

Using the created coordinate system as the Output Coordinate System, calculate the center of gravity (mm) of the assembly.

Another question could be - calculate the mass of the assembly in grams.

Provided Information:

Unit system: MMGS (millimeter, gram, second)

Decimal places: 2

Base1 part

BaseB part

Let's begin.

Replace the Base1 component in the Welding Arm assembly.

1. **Right-click** Base1 in the Assembly FeatureManager. Click **Replace Components**.

2. **Browse** to the location that you downloaded all of the needed models from the enclosed DVD (Segment 3 Initial/Initial 5 - replace base folder).

3. **Double-click** BaseB. Click **OK** from the PropertyManager.

The What's Wrong dialog box is displayed. Isolate the Base component. *This section presents a representation of the types of questions that you will see in this segment of the exam. Depending on your selection of faces and order of components inserted into the top level assembly, your error messages may vary. Address errors as needed.*

Replace the missing faces to address the mates errors.

4. **Click** Isolate. Click **Replacement Part Only (Selected Entity)**. The Base1 part is displayed in the isolate window. The BaseB part is displayed in the Graphics window.

5. **Click** the inside cylindrical face of BaseB as illustrated. The Concentric1 error is removed.

6. **Expand** the Face of BaseB-1 Mate Entities.

7. **Click** Coincident4.

8. **Click** inside the flat bottom circular face of BaseB as illustrated. The error is removed.

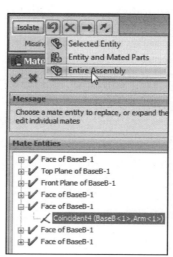

9. **Click** Entire Assembly from the Isolate box. The arm is in the correct orientation. If not, click the Flip Mate Alignment button.

10. **Click** OK from the Mated Entities PropertyManager. There is still an error with the coordinate system.

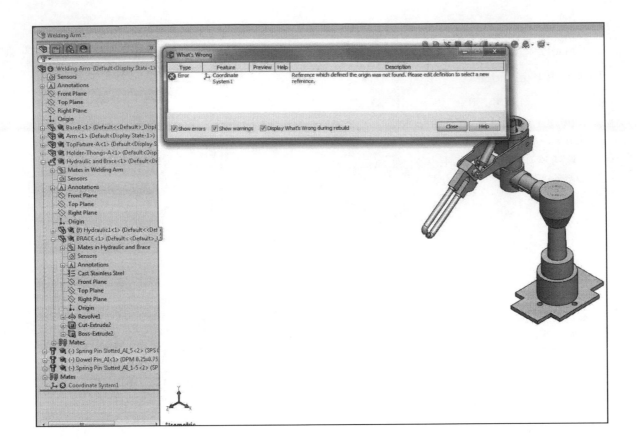

Confirm the position of the Arm component inside the Welding Arm assembly. Use the Change Transparency tool or a section view to confirm the location of mated components in the assembly.

11. **Right-click** Change Transparency from the BaseB component in the Assembly PropertyManager.

12. **Close** all dialog boxes.

Address the error for Coordinate System1. Redefine the vertex.

13. **Edit** Coordinate System1.

14. **Click** the bottom right front vertex on the BaseB component as illustrated.

15. **Calculate** the mass of the assembly in grams.

16. **Enter 5251.51** grams. Always enter the needed decimal places in the answer field.

17. **Calculate** the center of gravity (mm) relative to the redefined Coordinate System1. Enter the center of mass in the three blank fields in the exam.

   X = -87.30

   Y = 36.84

   Z = 130.27

18. **Save** the assembly.

In the exam you may see additional Mate errors.

Depending on your selection of faces and order of components inserted into the top level assembly, your error messages may vary. This guide is not designed to teach a new user how to use SolidWorks.

Segment 3 of the CSWP CORE exam - Additional Practice Problems

In this section, there are fewer step-by-step procedures then above. Use the provided initial and final models with the rollback bar if needed.

Create an assembly (Bench Vise) starting with the Bench Vise-Base component.

Some components in the exam are modeled by you and others will be supplied to you.

Load the Testing client and read the instructions. Create a folder to save your working models.

The first question in this segment is instructional.

The second question can be - download the Bench Vise-Base component and create the Bench Vise assembly.

Insert and orientate the Bench Vise-Base component as illustrated below with the Red tab in the front location.

Provided information:

Units: IPS (inch, pound, second)

Decimal Places: 2

Part Origin: Arbitrary

All holes through all unless shown otherwise.

There are no inferences.

The Top Plane of the assembly is perpendicular with the Front Plane of the Bench Vise-Base component.

*Isometric

Red tab location

Red tab location

*Isometric

What is the center of gravity of the Bench Vise-Base component in the assembly?

☀ SolidWorks will provide a part to create that is not orientated correctly in the assembly. Knowledge of component orientation in an assembly is required along with creating coordinate systems.

Let's begin.

1. **Create** an assembly document. Insert the Bench Vise-Base component (Segment 3 Initial/Bench Vise Parts folder). By default the Bench Vise-Base is fixed to the origin. Set document units and precision.

There are numerous ways to modify the orientation of a component in an assembly document that is fixed to the origin.

Use the Float and Mate tools in the next section. Re-orientate the Bench Vise-Base component. Fully define the component in the Assembly document.

2. **Float** the part. The part is free to translate or rotate in the Assembly document (six degrees of freedom).

3. **Re-orientate** the assembly as needed. Create a Coincident mate between the Right Plane of the Bench Vise-Base component and the Top Plane of the assembly.

4. **Click** the Aligned option if needed.

Create two additional Coincident mates.

5. **Create** a Coincident mate between the Right Plane of the Assembly and the Top Plane of the Bench Vise-Base component.

Another mate is needed to fully define the component.

6. **Create** a Coincident mate between the Front Plane of the Assembly and the Front Plane of the Bench Vise-Base component. The Bench Vise-Base component is fully defined in the Assembly document.

☀ You can also rotate the Bench Vise-Base component in the assembly using the Rotate Component tool (about Y&X). View the provided media files for additional information.

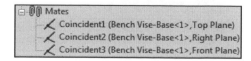

7. **Calculate** the center of gravity in inches of the Bench Vise-Base component in the assembly.

8. **Enter** the center of gravity in the three blank fields (inches). You need to be within 1% of the answer to get this question correct.

   X = 0.00

   Y = 0.59

   Z = 0.00

9. **Save** the assembly. In this example name the assembly Bench Vise.

SolidWorks Mass Properties calculates the center of mass for every model. At every instant of time, there is a unique location (x, y, z) in space that is the average position of the systems mass. The CSWP exam asks for center of gravity. For the purpose of calculating the center of mass and center of gravity near to earth or on earth, you can assume that the center of mass and the center of gravity are the same.

There are numerous ways to build the model in this section. A goal is to display different design intents and techniques.

Red tab location

Question 2:

A question in this segment could be - download and open the Bench Vise-Main Body sub assembly. Insert the Bench Vise-Main Body sub assembly into the Bench Vise assembly.

Position the Bench Vise-Main Body assembly with respect to the Bench Vise-Base component as illustrated.

All parts are Coincident and there are no inferences.

Insert all needed mates.

What is the center of gravity of the Bench Vise assembly?

Provided Information:

Unit system: IPS (inch, pound, second)

Decimal places: 2

SolidWorks provides symbols to indicate a Parallel mate, Width mate, Coincident mate, etc. in the exam.

Take your time to review the drawing views and to understand the required mates between each component.

In this example a Parallel mate is needed between the Front Plane of the Bench Vise-Main Body sub assembly and the Front Plane of the Bench Vise assembly.

Red tab location

*Isometric

Red tab location

Let's begin.

Insert the Bench Vise-Main Body sub assembly.

13. **Insert** the Bench Vise-Main Body sub assembly (from the Segment 3 Initial/Bench Vise Parts folder) into the Bench Vise assembly.

14. **Insert** a Coincident mate between the temporary axis of the Bench Vise-Base component and the temporary axis of the Bench Vise-Main Jaw Body sub assembly.

It is good practice to save frequently and to rename the part or assembly if you need to go back during the exam.

15. **Insert** a Coincident mate between the top face of the Bench Vise-Base component and the bottom face of the Bench Vise-Main body as illustrated. The Bench Vise is free to rotate.

Next restrict the rotation of the vise.

16. **Insert** a Parallel mate between the Front Plane of the Bench Vise-Main Body sub assembly and the Front Plane of the Bench Vise assembly.

17. **Calculate** the center of gravity of the Bench Vise assembly.

18. **Enter** the center of gravity (inch) in the three blank fields. You need to be within 1% of the answer to get this question correct.

X = -0.00

Y = 2.33

Z = 0.00

19. **Save** the assembly.

💡 You need to be within 1% of the answer to get this question correct.

💡 There are numerous ways to address the question in this section. A goal is to display different design intents and techniques.

💡 Quick mate is a new procedure in SW 2014 to mate components together in SolidWorks. No command (click Mate from the Assembly CommandManager) needs to be executed. Just make two selections (hold the Ctrl key down between selections) and a Quick Mate pop-up appears below the context toolbar. At this time, the quick mate procedure doesn't work on complex geometry.

Question 3:

A question in this segment could be - download and open the Bench Vise-Sliding Jaw and Bench Vise-Threaded rod component.

Insert the components into the Bench Vise assembly.

Calculate the Normal Distance (X) between the end face of the Bench Vise-Threaded rod to the back face of the Bench Vise-Threaded rod holder.

Insert a Distance mate between the face of the Bench Vise-Sliding Jaw and the face of the Bench Vise-Main Jaw body as illustrated.

The Front Plane of the assembly is parallel with the Front Plane of the Bench Vise Sliding Jaw component.

The Bench Vise-Threaded rod is free to rotate about its axis.

Bench Vise-Threaded rod

Bench Vise-Sliding Jaw

Front Plane

Red tab location

*Isometric

X

2.00

*Front

Provided Information:

Unit system: IPS (inch, pound, second)

Decimal places: 2

Let's begin.

20. **Insert** the Bench Vise-Sliding Jaw and the Bench Vise-Threaded rod (from the Segment 3 Initial/Bench Vise Parts folder) into the Bench Vise assembly.

21. **Insert** two Coincident mates to mate the Bench Vise-Sliding Jaw into the Bench Vise-Main jaw body.

22. **Insert** a Distance mate (2 inches) between the face of the Bench Vise-Sliding Jaw and the face of the Bench Vise-Main Jaw body jaws of the vise.

23. **Save** the assembly.

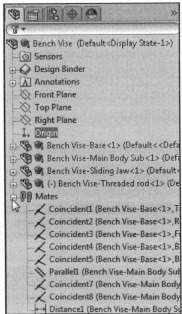

24. **Insert** a Coincident mate between the edge of the Bench Vise-Threaded rod and the hole edge of the Bench Vise-Sliding Jaw component as illustrated. The Bench Vise-Threaded rod is free to rotate about its axis.

Calculate the Normal Distance of X shown in the image. X is the distance from the end of the threaded rod to the back of the threaded rod holder.

25. **Apply** the Measure tool. Measure the distance between the end of the threaded rod to the back of the threaded rod holder.

26. **Enter 1.98** for the answer to this question. Always enter the needed decimal places in the answer field.

27. **Save** the assembly.

Question 4:

A question in this segment could be - download and open the Bench Vise Handle. Insert the Bench Vise Handle into the assembly. Mate the rod according to the below illustrations.

Red tab location

*Top

*Left

Bench Vise-Handle

*Right

To define the axial translation, apply the Move tool with Collision Detection to determine the position. The location is where the ball of the handle is Coincident with the hole in the threaded rod.

⚡ Knowledge of Collision Detection and the Measure tool is required for this section.

What is the center of gravity of the assembly?

Provided Information:

Unit system: IPS (inch, pound, second)

Decimal places: 2

Let's begin.

28. **Insert** the Bench Vise-Handle from the (Segment 3 Initial/Bench Vise Parts folder) into the Bench Vise assembly.

29. **Insert** a Concentric mate between the face of the hole of the threaded rod and the cylindrical face of the handle.

30. **Insert** an 80 degree Angle mate between the Right Plane of the Bench Vise-Handle and the Top Plane of the assembly. Apply the Flip Dimension option if needed.

31. **Activate** Collision detection from the Rotate Component PropertyManager. Locate where the Bench Vise-Handle will be coincident with the hole in the Bench Vise-Threaded rod. Note: You can also insert a Distance mate of 0.

32. **Calculate** the center of gravity of the assembly.

33. **Enter** the center of gravity in the three blank fields. You need to be within 1% of the answer to get this question correct. Always enter the needed decimal places in the answer field.

X = -1.86

Y = 2.85

Z = 0.03

34. **Save** the assembly.

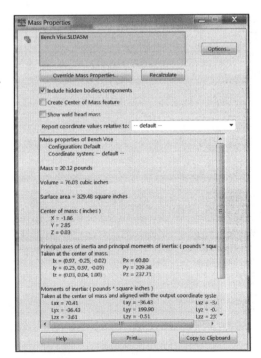

There are numerous ways to build the assembly in this section. A goal is to display different design intents and techniques.

Question 5:

A question in this segment could be - download and open the attached component Bench Vise-Base2.

Calculate the center of gravity in mm of the assembly relative to the location of the red tab location on the Bench Vise Base2 component.

Replace the Bench Vise-Base component with the Bench Vise-Base2 component.

Mate the Bench Vise to the Bench Vise-Base2 component using the same mates as with the Bench Vise-Base.

Maintain the same mates of the rest of the components as previously directed.

There are no interferences in the assembly.

Provided Information:

Unit system: MMGS (millimeter, gram, second)

Decimal places: 2

Bench Vise-Base

Bench Vise-Base2

Let's begin.

Replace the Bench Vise-Base component in the Bench Vise assembly.

1. **Right-click** Bench Vise-Base in the Assembly FeatureManager. Click Replace Components.

2. **Browse** to the location that you downloaded all of the needed models from the enclosed DVD (Segment 3 Initial/Bench Vise Parts folder).

3. **Double-click** Bench Vise-Base1. Click OK from the Replace PropertyManager.

Unselect the Re-attach mates box in the Replace PropertyManager to manually address all needed mates.

The What's Wrong dialog box is displayed. Isolate the Base component. *This section presents a representation of the types of questions that you will see in this segment of the exam. Depending on your selection of faces and order of components inserted into the top level assembly, your error messages may vary. Address errors as needed.*

Replace the missing faces to address the mate errors.

4. **Click** Isolate. Select Entity and Mated Parts.

5. **Delete** the mate between the Top Plane of the Bench Vise-Base 2 component (Concident2) and the Right Plane of the assembly.

6. **Modify** the Coincident mate that is currently with the Right Plane of the Bench Vise-Base2 and the Top Plane of the assembly to the Top Plane of the Bench Vise-Base2 component with the Top Plane of the assembly.

7. **Expand** the second Mate Entity error as illustrated.

8. **Click** Coincident5. It has a missing reference with the top face of Bench Vise-Base. Select the Top face of Bench Vise-Base 2.

9. **Expand** the first Mate Entity error.

10. **Click** Coincident4. Replace the missing reference. Select the temporary axis of Bench Vise-Base 2.

11. **Click** OK from the Mated Entities PropertyManager.

12. **Insert** a mate between the Right Plane of the Bench Vise-Base2 and the Right Plane of the assembly. The model is fully constrained.

13. **Modify** the assembly documents to MMGS.

14. **Calculate** the center of gravity in mm of the assembly relative to the location of the red tab location on the Bench Vise Base2 component.

Red tab location

15. **Enter** the center of gravity (mm) in the three blank fields. You need to be within 1% of the answer to get this question correct.

X = -40.13

Y = 79.94

Z = 0.67

16. **Save** the assembly. Note: Check the interference between the Bench Vise-Handle (Coincident) and the hole in the Bench Vise-Threaded rod if you are off in the Z direction.

You need to be within 1% of the answer to get this question correct.

There are numerous ways to address the question in this section. A goal is to display different design intents and techniques.

You are finished with this section. Good luck on segment 3 of the CSWP exam.

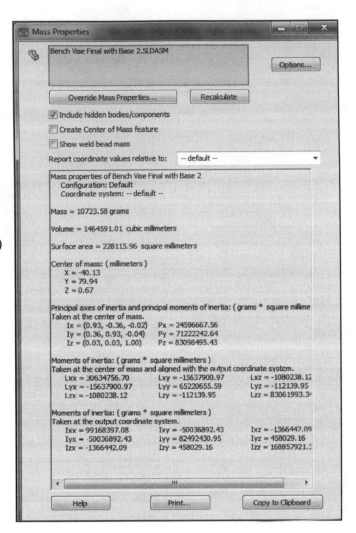

Mass Properties

Bench Vise Final with Base 2.SLDASM

Options...

Override Mass Properties...   Recalculate

☑ Include hidden bodies/components
☐ Create Center of Mass feature
☐ Show weld bead mass

Report coordinate values relative to: -- default --

Mass properties of Bench Vise Final with Base 2
    Configuration: Default
    Coordinate system: -- default --

Mass = 10723.58 grams

Volume = 1464591.01 cubic millimeters

Surface area = 228115.96 square millimeters

Center of mass: (millimeters)
    X = -40.13
    Y = 79.94
    Z = 0.67

Principal axes of inertia and principal moments of inertia: (grams * square millime
Taken at the center of mass.
    Ix = (0.93, -0.36, -0.02)   Px = 24596667.56
    Iy = (0.36, 0.93, -0.04)   Py = 71222242.64
    Iz = (0.03, 0.03, 1.00)   Pz = 83098495.43

Moments of inertia: (grams * square millimeters)
Taken at the center of mass and aligned with the output coordinate system.
    Lxx = 30634756.70   Lxy = -15637900.97   Lxz = -1080238.12
    Lyx = -15637900.97   Lyy = 65220655.59   Lyz = -112139.95
    Lzx = -1080238.12   Lzy = -112139.95   Lzz = 83061993.34

Moments of inertia: (grams * square millimeters)
Taken at the output coordinate system.
    Ixx = 99168397.08   Ixy = -50036892.43   Ixz = -1366442.09
    Iyx = -50036892.43   Iyy = 82492430.95   Iyz = 458029.16
    Izx = -1366442.09   Izy = 458029.16   Izz = 168857921.3

Help   Print...   Copy to Clipboard

Red tab location

At the end of the exam, view the Summary dialog box. Press the End Examination button only if you are finished.

A total score of 140 out of 190 or better is required to pass the third segment. When you pass the third segment of the CSWP CORE exam you will receive the following email. Click on the SolidWorks Certification Center hyperlink to login, activate and view your certificate.

Congratulations David!

You have been issued a certificate in SolidWorks® Virtual Test Center indicating that you have successfully completed the requirements for **Segment 3 of Certified SolidWorks Professional Core.**

CertificateID:

Visit your certificate area on SolidWorks® Certification Center. Click My Account to access your certificates and exams.

Congratulations,
Avelino Rochino

If you fail a segment of the exam, you need to wait 14 days until you can retake that segment. In that time, you can take another segment that you might not have taken until then.

Always save your models to verify your results.

There are numerous ways to address the question in this section. A goal is to display different design intents and techniques.

The images displayed on the exam are not to scale due to differences in the parts being downloaded for each tester.

SolidWorks will provide a part to create in this segment that is not orientated correctly in the assembly. Knowledge of component orientation in an assembly is required along with creating a new coordinate system.

Notes:

Appendix

SolidWorks Keyboard Shortcuts

Listed below are some of the pre-defined keyboard shortcuts in SolidWorks:

Action:	Key Combination:
Model Views	
Rotate the model horizontally or vertically:	**Arrow** keys
Rotate the model horizontally or vertically 90 degrees.	**Shift** + **Arrow** keys
Rotate the model clockwise or counterclockwise	**Alt** + left of right **Arrow** keys
Pan the model	**Ctrl** + **Arrow** keys
Magnifying glass	**g**
Zoom in	**Shift** + **z**
Zoom out	**z**
Zoom to fit	**f**
Previous view	**Ctrl** + **Shift** + **z**
View Orientation	
View Orientation menu	**Spacebar**
Front view	**Ctrl** + **1**
Back view	**Ctrl** + **2**
Left view	**Ctrl** + **3**
Right view	**Ctrl** + **4**
Top view	**Ctrl** + **5**
Bottom view	**Ctrl** + **6**
Isometric view	**Ctrl** + **7**
NormalTo view	**Ctrl** + **8**
Selection Filters	
Filter edges	**e**
Filter vertices	**v**
Filter faces	**x**
Toggle Selection Filter toolbar	**F5**
Toggle selection filters on/off	**F6**
File menu items	
New SolidWorks document	**Ctrl** + **n**
Open document	**Ctrl** + **o**
Open From Web Folder	**Ctrl** + **w**
Make Drawing from Part	**Ctrl** + **d**
Make Assembly from Part	**Ctrl** + **a**
Save	**Ctrl** + **s**
Print	**Ctrl** + **p**
Additional shortcuts	
Access online help inside of PropertyManager or dialog box	**F1**

Rename an item in the FeatureManager design tree	**F2**
Rebuild the model	**Ctrl + b**
Force rebuild – Rebuild the model and all its features	**Ctrl + q**
Redraw the screen	**Ctrl + r**
Cycle between open SolidWorks document	**Ctrl + Tab**
Line to arc/arc to line in the Sketch	**a**
Undo	**Ctrl + z**
Redo	**Ctrl + y**
Cut	**Ctrl + x**
Copy	**Ctrl + c**
Additional shortcuts	
Paste	**Ctrl + v**
Delete	**Delete**
Next window	**Ctrl + F6**
Close window	**Ctrl + F4**
View previous tools	**s**
Selects all text inside an Annotations text box	**Ctrl + a**

In a sketch, the **Esc** key un-selects geometry items currently selected in the Properties box and Add Relations box. In the model, the **Esc** key closes the PropertyManager and cancels the selections.

Use the **g** key to activate the Magnifying glass tool. Use the Magnifying glass tool to inspect a model and make selections without changing the overall view.

Use the **s** key to view/access previous command tools in the Graphics window.

SolidWorks Document Types

SolidWorks has three main document file types: Part, Assembly and Drawing, but there are many additional supporting types that you may want to know. Below is a brief list of these supporting file types:

Design Documents	**Description**
.sldprt	SolidWorks Part document
.slddrw	SolidWorks Drawing document
.sldasm	SolidWorks Assembly document

Templates and Formats	**Description**
.asmdot	Assembly Template
.asmprp	Assembly Template Custom Properties tab
.drwdot	Drawing Template
.drwprp	Drawing Template Custom Properties tab
.prtdot	Part Template
.prtprp	Part Template Custom Properties tab
.sldbt	General Table Template
.slddrt	Drawing Sheet Template
.sldbombt	Bill of Materials Template (Table-based)
.sldholtbt	Hole Table Template
.xls	Bill of Materials Template (Excel)

Library Files	**Description**
.sldlfp	Library Part file
.sldblk	Blocks

Other	**Description**
.sldstd	Drafting standard
.sldmat	Material Database
.sldclr	Color Palette File

Helpful On-Line Information

The SolidWorks URL: http://www.solidworks.com contains information on Local Resellers, Solution Partners, Certifications, SolidWorks users groups, and more.

Access 3D ContentCentral using the Task Pane to obtain engineering electronic catalog model and part information.

Use the SolidWorks Resources tab in the Task Pane to obtain access to Customer Portals, Discussion Forums, User Groups, Manufacturers, Solution Partners, Labs and more.

Helpful on-line SolidWorks information is available from the following URLs:

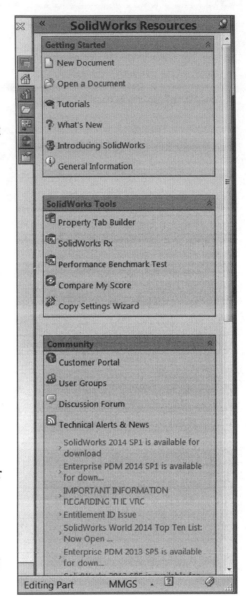

- http://www.dmeducation.net

  Helpful tips, tricks and what's new.

- http://www.solidworks.com/sw/engineering-education-software.htm

  SolidWorks in Academia. Information on software, support, tutorials, blog and more.

- http://www.solidworks.com/sw/support/engineering-certification.htm

  Frequently Asked Questions on the SolidWorks Certification Programs.

- http://www.solidworks.com/sw/support/797_ENU_HTML.htm

  Certified SolidWorks Professional exam information.

*On-line tutorials are for educational purposes only. Tutorials are copyrighted by their respective owners.

Index